The Biggest Fight

Michael
Watson.

TIME WARNER BOOKS UK

ABACUS · LITTLE, BROWN · ORBIT · TIME WARNER BOOKS · VIRAGO PRESS

The Biggest Fight

MICHAEL WATSON'S STORY

MICHAEL WATSON
with STEVE BUNCE

timewarner
books

A *Time Warner* Book

First published in Great Britain in 2004 by Time Warner Books
Reprinted 2004

ISBN 0 316 72564 1

Typeset in Sabon by M Rules
Printed and bound in Great Britain
by Clays Ltd, St Ives plc

Time Warner Books
An imprint of
Time Warner Book Group UK
Brettenham House
Lancaster Place
London WC2E 7EN

www.twbg.co.uk

*For my mother
and
for my daughters
Jamilla and Layla*

Foreword

Michael Watson's injury not only changed his life forever, but those of countless others. It resulted in improved safety provisions for all those competing in British sport, increased the funding for brain and spine research, and gave hope to the thousands of people affected by brain and spinal disorders. He is a man whose ability in the face of such horrendous adversity has inspired us all.

I was among those blessed to walk with him on the six-day triumph that was his Flora London Marathon. After all that suffering, I asked him why he was willing to take part in the marathon. He replied, 'Peter, it is for people less fortunate than me.' In so saying, he summed up what his awesome journey has meant. Michael has done far more for me spiritually than I have ever been able to do for him physically. He is a man who has given more to the world than he has taken. A man who, to this day, carries a burden that would extinguish most of us and yet continues to be a brilliant beacon of joy and hope.

Peter J Hamlyn MB, BS, BSc, MD FRCS, FISM
Consultant Neurosurgeon to St Bartholomew's and
The Royal London Hospital, 2004

Acknowledgements

I give thanks to God for my life, and to my dear mother, Joan, for being a constant source of love and strength. My brother Jeffrey and Uncle Joe have always been there for me, and, as a family, we have all been supported by the members of Evering Pentecostal Church. Lennard Ballack, a true friend who is more like a brother to me, is a great help and never far from my side.

Special thanks to Peter Hamlyn, the neurosurgical team and all at St Bartholomew's Hospital who helped save my life.

Thanks and deep gratitude to all at Homerton Hospital, the Brain and Spine Foundation and Headway, and all the countless other professionals or volunteers who helped with my recovery and rehabilitation. I owe much to my carers, especially Richard Humphrey, for all their understanding and support.

My thanks to my editor Elise Dillsworth for her care and dedication, and without whom this book would not have been possible.

My appreciation and thanks to Michael Toohig and everyone at Myers, Fletcher & Gordon, and to my agent Geraldine Davies for all the help they have given me.

I am deeply grateful to all those who gave their time to contribute to this book and help fill in the details.

And thanks to the public for all the support you have shown me over the years.

God bless you all.

Chapter 1

My mum, Joan, grew up in Jamaica, but in 1964, a young woman of twenty, she got on a plane to London to follow my dad in search of a new beginning.

She had no idea how her life would turn out when she arrived. At first they lived in a small flat in Stamford Hill in north London. Mum had a deep belief in God, so finding a church was important to her in a foreign land where she had very few friends. She found one in Tottenham and attended regularly. This helped her to settle in to her new life.

Mum and Dad were married in 1964. My dad, Jim, had found a job in Enfield at a chemical company, and he kept the same job until he retired. Mum found a job too, but she left after a short while when she realised she was pregnant. My parents were both industrious and desperate to give their future family a good start in the new city they had chosen.

By the time I was born, my parents were renting a two-bedroom flat in Rectory Road, Stoke Newington. Mum had put our names down on the local council's books, but there was a long wait. We were on the council's list nearly ten years before we moved into a permanent flat.

I appeared on the morning of 15 March 1965 at Mother's Hospital, Clapton. I was a very soft child, very gentle, and my mum remembers that I would cry at anything. She has also told me again and again that when I was a baby I looked like a little girl, with big dark eyes and long lashes.

On Sundays I would be wrapped in blankets and taken to the Crescent Pentecostal church in Tottenham for a day of spiritual rejoicing. I would suck on a dummy if I was unhappy or teething or sick. I reached my first birthday on my mum's lap, gently rocking to and fro to the hymns and prayers and salutations of the devoted flock of West Indian immigrants. I also heard the preacher's thunder from the pulpit during those early days. It seems I grew up listening to believers talking to non-believers in churches and living rooms before I could read or write.

When I was still only a baby, I was dropped off with a nanny for a time as my mum had managed to get a job at an old people's home. Mum always worked when she could because that is what her parents back in Jamaica had taught her, but when I was little more than a year old Mum was pregnant again, so she stopped working and we spent a lot of time together at the flat in Rectory Road. Dad was working long and late hours at the Enfield factory, and Mum was running our lives in the small flat. Life, I guess, was fairly normal and very happy.

My brother Jeffrey was born at Mother's Hospital, Clapton, on 22 May 1967. He was then, and remains, my little brother, but later in life he would spend a few years playing big brother to me. It is not hard to imagine just how happy Mum was with her two boys. Our swift arrival must have helped her cope with leaving her first child, Dawn, in Jamaica with her parents, though she kept in touch.

Even though Mum had her boys and my dad had his job, we did not lead a life of luxury or leisure at our small Rectory Road flat. There was lots of love but never enough money, and after Jeff was born Mum had to quickly go back to work at the old people's home. Each morning Jeff would be tucked away warmly inside his pram and I would be lifted into the seat that is strapped over the pram's cover. Mum would push us to the nanny's house off Stamford Hill and then go and do a day's work.

One evening in January Mum picked us up from the nanny's flat. It was freezing cold and Mum had been at work all day. I was on top of the blue Silver Cross pram, and Jeff was inside. As she waited at a crossing on Stamford Hill near the junction with Cazenove Road, a bus came slowly to a halt. She stayed on the pavement even when the driver motioned for her to walk. She waited as he put his arm out of the window and indicated to the traffic on his outside to slow down, waited a few seconds more, and then carefully pushed the pram on to the crossing. It took her a few steps to get clear of the bus.

She managed just one more step before a car crashed into the pram and it was wrenched from her hands. The car had ignored the hand signal from the bus driver and had carried on regardless. Mum ended up on her hands and knees on the road with just a few scrapes and bruises. I was thrown from the chair and hurt my knees when I landed. I ended up under a parked car, but I was fine. Jeff took the full impact of the car and was thrown from the safety of his pram.

One eyewitness later told Mum that all three of us had been thrown through the air, and the woman admitted that she thought all three of us were dead. The pram was crumpled and the wheels had been knocked clean off. It was a scene of carnage and people rushed from shops and cars to see if there was anything they could do.

Jeff was not as lucky as me. When Mum had recovered from the initial shock of having the pram yanked from her hands, she ran over to where Jeff was. He was unconscious, and the fight to save his life had started.

An ambulance arrived and Mum, Jeff and I were rushed off to the Prince of Wales hospital. Mum and I were examined and cleaned up, but elsewhere in the hospital doctors were taking X-rays and trying to find out just how seriously hurt Jeff was. He was eight months old and in a coma; for Mum every mother's nightmare was about to begin.

Jeff had suffered a serious head injury but he was simply too small for the surgeons to operate. His life was in the balance, and after three days he was given his last rites. By that time I had been taken from the hospital and was staying with members of Sister Paris's church in Clapton, Mum's replacement family.

When Sister Paris found out about the last rites, she arrived at the bedside in the fiery manner of a Pentecostal preacher on a mission to save a soul. She took control at the side of the bed and besieged everyone, demanding that they pray to save Jeff. She knelt and prayed that afternoon with Mum and Dad. They prayed for my brother not to die, and Sister Paris prayed loud and clear for a miracle.

Jeff held stubbornly on to life during four months in a coma. He was in hospital for my second birthday and for his first birthday. He finally came round. If you meet Jeff today you will notice that he drags his left side a bit and slurs his words, but he set the precedent for recovery in my family. His accident was a warm-up for Mum, though nobody could have predicted then that she would have to go through it all again with me twenty years later.

When Jeff was released, Mum had to take him all over North London to different hospitals for specialist treatment. The driver of the car that hit the pram was prosecuted for not stopping. My Mum has done her best to erase the memory of the crash – she has no idea what happened to the driver. All she was bothered about was getting Jeff out of hospital and back to the flat in Rectory Road. In that flat we were a family again and life returned to normal, with Dad away a lot of the time working in Enfield. I was the big brother and I had to look after Jeff when we played together on the living-room floor.

During the months after Jeff's release from hospital in 1968 Mum developed an extra sense that alerted her if ever her boys needed her. The crash had scared her, and from that point on she was determined to keep both of her sons safe and never take a risk with us.

A small child or baby with a brain injury has even less chance of communicating than an adult, but Mum always seemed to know when Jeff needed something or was in pain. It was the same with me when I was stuck inside the silence that resulted from the brain injury. Mum could read my eyes just like she read Jeff's.

Our flat in Rectory Road, Stoke Newington, was in a three-storey house in a mixed neighbourhood in a part of north London that was constantly changing. We lived in the middle flat and another two families lived below and above us. It was a happy community, busy with activity and the usual noise from young families.

In 1969, a year after Jeff's accident, he was recovering well but he still needed a lot of care and regular visits to different hospitals for assessments. I played with him all the time because I knew it would help with his recovery. He was my baby brother and to me he was just a normal kid. I would go with Mum and Jeff on their hospital visits – long days with several changes of bus and endless waiting. I was only small, but I can remember just how grey and cold the buildings looked and felt. None of them had changed over twenty years later when I ended up in a similar type of recovery unit. I've always had a bad feeling about old hospitals and dark hallways and I'm sure that comes from the many times I went with Mum and Jeff.

One night at the flat, as Jeff and I played in the living room and watched the television, I could smell something. I had no idea where it was coming from, but I knew that it was not one of the normal smells that often filled the flat and the staircases in the rest of the house, like chicken cooking or Mum's special stew. It was one that I had never experienced before, and it was getting stronger and stronger. I was only four but I knew it was odd and dangerous in some way.

I called out to Mum but it was difficult for her to hear me above the noise of the television and the usual smashing and crashing from the kitchen. Eventually, after calling out a few times, I got up and walked over to the kitchen door. Mum was singing to herself as she prepared our food. I can remember part of the hymn and I am always struck by the relevance of the words.

Your grace and mercy has brought me through,
I'm living this moment because of you.

Mum is a great cook and had started to get a reputation. She always said the two things she brought with her from Jamaica were her religion and her cooking skills.

I could see the steam rising from the top of the stove and on the surfaces the various plates were piled high with food. She would prepare chicken, rice and peas, dumplings, cornmeal porridge and sweet potato. I took my eyes off the food and called her again. This time she heard me, stopped singing and turned round to look at me with surprise in her eyes.

'What's up, Michael? Where's Jeffrey?' she asked.

I told her that I could smell something strange. She grabbed my hand and walked out of the kitchen with me, then she could smell it and she knew it was smoke from a fire. She had no idea where it was coming from, but she knew it was a bad situation when she walked into the living room.

She told us to stay on the floor in front of the TV and went to the doors that led to the two bedrooms. First she opened our door and there was nothing in there. Then she turned the handle on her door and instantly heard the 'whooshing' noise that everybody discovering a house fire can remember. She quickly closed the door to keep the black smoke out of the living area. She knew then that she had to get her two boys out of the house and to safety, and quickly.

She rushed across the room to where Jeffrey and I were sitting on the floor and picked us up, and then we were all heading for the door. We never stopped to get anything – Mum ran straight out of the flat and down the stairs to the street, shouting 'Fire, fire, get out, get out.'

Mum took us out of the front door on to the street. Behind us I could hear people shouting and doors opening and closing as panic took over. I can remember feeling scared because I still had no idea what was really happening, even when I saw the smoke start to drift out from the open door.

Mum took us across the road and we turned to look back at the house. By now men, women and children from the other two families were running out of the door. Some had grabbed a few items but I don't think anybody stayed to recover much because it was obvious from Mum's voice and the smoke that the situation was serious. There was a lot of shouting between Mum and the other adults, and some neighbours in the busy street had started to look out of their windows. One of the women from a house a few doors down took Jeff from Mum and she wanted to take me, but I refused to leave Mum's side.

Somebody had called the fire brigade and I could hear the sirens somewhere in the distance. I just stood next to Mum, holding her hand and listening as neighbours came over and chatted and asked what had happened. I heard Mum tell people that I had been the one to smell the fire. There were a lot of adults, neighbours that I had seen and some that I had never seen, and they were all on the pavement, just standing and looking back at the house.

I looked over and could now see why they were all staring – there was a volcano coming out of the front window in the middle flat. The flames and smoke were spreading quickly. Soon the room where Jeff and I had been playing in just a few minutes earlier was on fire.

The fire brigade arrived and soon blocked the road off, and in a flash the two engines and dozens of men swarmed all over to try and put the blaze out. I can remember thinking that it was very exciting as I stood and watched. I held Mum's hand as our home burned in front of our eyes. Mum was by now surrounded by a lot of familiar faces – I recognised women from Mum's church, the Sister Paris in Clapton, and other people that I had seen in the flat at various times. Mum often cooked for other families and some of the women had been to the house to collect food. Everybody seemed very concerned for us, but Mum seemed as strong then as I can ever remember her being. She told me many years later that a great fear gripped her that night because she realised just how close she had come to losing her boys. She was not crying and screaming because she had us and she was safe, but I can guess at the enormous sense of relief she felt.

I watched as the flames were slowly put out and the black and smelly smoke from the old furniture filled the air in the street. The volcano was gone and the firemen started to move in and out of the smoking house. I guess I expected them to come out with an armful of my favourite toys but they dragged out filthy mattresses and sofas instead and threw them on to the pavement. The house was gutted and none of the families could salvage much from the wreck of the flames.

Mum lost all of her pictures of Jeff and me, and to this day she has only managed to get a few together by asking relatives to give her back any that she had sent them. As a father, I now realise just how hard that must have been because I've got my own children and I love the pictures I have of them. At my mum's flat in Islington there are pictures of me with my two daughters, but none of Jeff and me, which reminds me of what my mum lost that night in the fire.

On that night the pictures were far from Mum's mind because the most important thing was we were all safe. Once again her faith had pulled her through, with just a little bit of help from my nose! Mum always tells people that God put it in me to raise the alarm and save everybody in that house. I thank God for saving us that night.

The police arrived and joined the rest of the people watching the flames. Soon, however, they naturally started to ask questions about the fire and where it had started. Mum told them that I had been the first to smell the fire and that it had started in her bedroom. Mum thinks it was the old paraffin heater, which was how we all kept warm during the cold, damp winter months. She thinks the heater tipped over, or something fell on it earlier in the evening, and then the fire spread. Later that night the fireman told Mum that most house fires started that way.

There were just a few people left on the street by the time the fire brigade had finished dragging out the smouldering furniture, and we all looked at what remained of 64 Rectory Road. It was the only home that I had ever known and now it was gone.

One of the women with Mum on the pavement was Doris White, and she stood and listened as the police told us that we would be put in a local bed and breakfast for the night. I think Mum knew what type of hostel we would end up in and I know she was not looking forward to taking her boys there.

'Sister Joan,' she said to my mum, 'you can come and stay with us.'

It was settled there and then, and she went off to phone her husband to come and get us from the street.

Uncle Joe arrived not long after she made the call. I knew him already from his visits to the flat and from our visits to the same church that he took his wife and six children to, but on that dark and cold night when he pulled up in a van it was the start of a special relationship between us. He was not my dad, but at times he was even more than a dad. I treated him like a dad and he has always said that he thought of me as a son.

Uncle Joe climbed out from the driving seat to greet everybody on the pavement. He knew the women who had gathered to comfort and offer support to Mum from the church in Clapton. They all respected him for his beliefs and his faith, and he would eventually have his own church. Back then he was a very charismatic man, and even now, in his seventies, there remains something special about him.

In the early fifties Uncle Joe arrived in Britain from Montserrat in the West Indies. He was part of the first wave of West Indians to arrive in Britain for a better life with more opportunities than the life they had left behind in the Caribbean. Uncle Joe could turn his hand to anything, and he often had to during his first few years in Britain when he struggled to make ends meet.

'Michael, a man has to work,' he would always tell me.

He drove coaches all over the country and also worked for Customs and Excise at Heathrow airport. He had a varied and entertaining life, but the most amazing tale he told was the night he found God while he was in bed at his house in Evering Road, Stoke Newington.

It was just a normal night, but Uncle Joe was having trouble sleeping. He was thinking about all the things he had to do when he heard a voice.

'Stop, Joe.'

The way Uncle Joe tells the story has not changed much over the years. When he heard the voice he looked over his shoulder to see if somebody was behind his bed, but he knew he was on his own. He also knew immediately where the voice had come from. Uncle Joe got out of bed and fell to his knees. He stayed down on his knees and prayed. He offered himself to God on that carpet that night and he has never looked back.

Uncle Joe knew that he needed to find a church and find it quickly, because from that moment his old life was over and he wanted to give his new life to God. He went out into the street and unlocked the door to his car and drove until he found a Pentecostal church, which was the only kind of church he knew because back in Montserrat he had seen Pentecostal churches when he was younger. Uncle Joe had not been religious until the night he fell from bed and dropped to his knees.

Eventually he found a church and tracked down the pastor and, as he tells it, arrived at the pastor's door at midnight. The man opened his door and didn't seem surprised that Uncle Joe was standing there. Uncle Joe told the pastor what had happened and they prayed. He became a devoted member of the church and eventually started to preach himself. It was shortly after his conversion that Uncle Joe met my mum and dad.

That night in Rectory Road was not the first or last time that I came close to death. Looking back at the fire, I realise that I'm a man with a destiny and a purpose. The fire and other things happened for a reason. They made me become the man I am today. God gave me my life back so that I could give to others. I know that now, but on that dark night in Rectory Road I was just a little boy holding on to my Mum's hand and never wanting to let go as we watched our small flat burn.

Later that night, after we had all settled in at Uncle Joe's in Dalston, my dad finally appeared. He had been at his job in Enfield and had been unaware of what had happened.

We finally left Uncle Joe's house and moved to 43 Forest Road, Dalston after ten months. The new flat was just a temporary home until the council could put us somewhere permanently. After surviving Jeffrey's accident and the fire as a family, living in a temporary home was not much of a hardship.

In 1970 I started at Queensbridge primary school, which was very close to the flat. Each day Mum would take me there and then she would put Jeff on a bus that came to the flat and took him off to a school for people with special needs. Mum would go to work at a nursing home in Dalston.

On my first day at Queensbridge I met a boy called Ray Webb and although we never fought in the playground, many years later we trained together at Colvestone gym. Ray became my sparring partner and once actually broke my nose.

There were times when Mum was stuck at work and somebody else, usually one of the sisters from the church, would pick me up. However, Mum would always cook a full meal when she arrived home. She worked long hours and never had any private time, and that is one of the main reasons that the church was so important to her. Each weekend she would dress up and involve herself in various church functions and affairs over both days. There always seemed to be something happening, and it has never changed. My dad was never really a big part of it, and he would stay at home with Jeff when Mum took me. Although he had occasionally gone to church when he and Mum first got married, the fascination had faded, and even though he was a close friend of Uncle Joe I think he found their religious fervour too strong. He worked even longer hours and was never as influential as Mum was in our upbringing.

The council finally found us a permanent home three years later in 1973, a new flat in St. Aubin's Court on the De Beauvoir Estate on the edge of Islington and Dalston. It was less than half a mile from the flat in Forest Road, and it felt like a proper home from the very start. I would have to change schools and move from Queensbridge to the Whitmore Road school, but that was easy.

At the new school it was easy to make friends because so many of the boys lived in the same flats. There were the Pattersons, Ronald, Crooksy and Leyton. We would play together on the street and on the small bit of grass near the flats. But it was at the flats that I made a significant friendship with a boy called Lennard Ballack. Our families were friendly, and my brother Jeffrey spent a lot of time with Lennard. Over the years, Lennard and I became close, and he has selflessly given me, and continues to give, a lot of help and support. As a true friend he has been there through the good times and the bad.

Mum, Jeffrey and I would make the short journey to the church as many as three times each week. Mum would have her hat on and Jeffrey and I would have on our best clothes, which often led to a few comments from my friends back at the flats. They would call out to me, 'Hey, Sunday School Boy.' When I was a bit older they changed the name and called me 'Pastor Watson'. But as my mum would always say, 'Only the best is good enough for God'.

Uncle Joe was now part of the family and was a regular visitor to our new flat. He got on very well with Mum and Dad and was very good to Jeffrey and me.

Life at St. Aubin's Court was good and I enjoyed school. I always like to dress smart and would make trips to the West End to go shopping. I was surrounded by a loving family and a lot of friends. I would play football and cricket whenever I got the chance.

At eleven I went to Daneford School in Bethnal Green, which was again not far from where we lived. It was a big school. I was growing up fast, but Mum and Uncle Joe thought I needed to 'tough up' a bit. Actually school was never a problem for me because I kept quiet and tried to stay clear of trouble and confrontation.

I was quiet and very shy. I had few close friends and liked to keep my own company, apart from when I was playing games. But nothing rough. I was never a fighting kid. No one, least of all me, realised what fight I had in me.

Chapter 2

At fourteen I decided that I wanted to box. I had watched Muhammad Ali and Roberto Duran on TV and I liked their style and their temperament. The boxing gym was not far from the flat, but for me each short walk became part of a longer journey.

I first went looking for a form of self-defence. Shortly before I joined the club I was involved in a scrape with an older and bigger boy that had left my pride bruised if my face intact. I knew that Mum was right when she said that I needed to 'tough up', but that was more to do with me being nice than me being 'soft'. However, I wanted to learn how to defend myself if I ever had to.

I was a member at Crown and Manor before I started to use its boxing gym. I did athletics and was really committed to it. But as soon as I was inside the ring with the gloves on, I realised this was my destiny. It seemed I had a natural talent for throwing a punch. And it was a boy from the flats who led me to this discovery.

One day we were playing football and I scored the winning goal. This boy was a bad loser, so he came up to me and started calling me names, and telling me that I should be at church praying, not playing football. When he pushed me I started to retaliate, I thought enough is enough. But I was no match for him and he beat me up! I realised then I had to learn to defend myself and headed for a boxing gym.

I was sharp enough and quick enough to learn some essential rules from the very start. I worked out long before I became a decent amateur boxer that the most important thing inside the ring was hitting, not getting hit. From the start I could hit the other boy with a clean and accurate punch and not get hit. I could stand up right and put together jabs and a few other punches from the earliest days, and as I was taught more and more I just absorbed everything. It was all coming together, and each night back at the flat I would shadow-box and put myself through endless hours of moving and punching.

As soon as I started boxing I knew I had found the perfect way to express myself. I felt I had a gift from God and that I had natural talent in the boxing ring, and to add to that I was a born entertainer.

After a few weeks in the gym I was finally allowed to spar, something I had been waiting for patiently. In front of the bags and on the pads I could hit the target with a list of different punches. I could land jabs and hooks, short rights, right uppercuts and move in and out easily. I enjoyed sparring even better. I always felt in control and dominant. I liked demonstrating my potential, showing off my skill, and I loved the reaction from people watching.

I had about twenty fights at Crown and Manor and I think I only lost twice. Bob Kipps and Eric Whistler, who ran the boxing club, can't remember me losing more than twice, and both of those were important fights. The first loss was at the Bloomsbury Crest hotel in May 1981 in the Junior Amateur Boxing Association final at Class B under-71 kilos. It was my first final, and at sixteen I really thought I was something special. In the gym and the ring until that time I had been in control, and my right hand could end most fights. That night, thinking I was the star of the show, I lost on points to Currock House's Garry Sanderson. It was still a close fight, but the lesson was simple – never be too confident.

Perhaps the worst part of the defeat was that the Bloomsbury Crest hotel was about two miles from where I was living. That hit me hard because I had a lot of supporters in the packed hall, including some from Mum's congregation. It was reassuring to have them there and I didn't want to disappoint them.

My brother Jeff never came to any of my fights because he didn't like to see me get hurt. And my dad only saw me fight once. But Uncle Joe came to most of them and spurred me on and always kept cool because he had confidence in me. Mum never had a problem with my fights because she knew that I was more than able to look after myself. She worried more about the opponent who was on the receiving end. I'd learned my lesson good and fast.

The loss in the Junior ABA finals was, sadly, to prove not quite enough of a wake-up call for me. In December 1981 I travelled with Eric and Bob to Milton Keynes for the National Association of Boys Clubs Class B semi-final. I had a kid called R. Connor from New Addington. I had no idea where New Addington was, but I quickly found out that R. Connor was in fact Roy Connor, a previous champion when he was with a different club. The surprises didn't stop there. At the weigh-in we all realised that Connor had joined the Fitzroy Lodge club in Lambeth, South London and he had Mick Carney, one of the amateur sport's legendary trainers, in his corner.

I lost that night because I had no idea how to deal with Connor's southpaw style and timing. I was used to opponents jabbing with their left, but Connor used his right. He knew enough to let me miss and counter and glide away in what was no doubt a dull fight to watch but a superb boxing lesson of the highest order. I had more power and I was fit, but I had no luck in that ring against such a superior fighter. Also, I was too confident going into the fight. But even if I had been more respectful, I would probably have lost. I needed an extra edge to my boxing game, and I knew the right place to get it.

I was just seventeen when I decided that dominating the ring at Crown and Manor was never going to help me get where I wanted to be. I was wise enough to realise that I needed to be tested or my progress would stop.

I made a move to the Colvestone gym in Hackney, and from the start it was obvious that the place was very different. There was a mix of professionals and amateurs here, so I had the opportunity to spar with seasoned fighters. There were more rounds and they lasted longer, so I could take the time to develop my skills. I made sure that I left my old club on good terms and even popped in there from time to time.

The two gyms were less than two miles apart, but in boxing terms it was a serious distance from one ring to the other. I was a boy when I first walked into the Crown and Manor, but I became a man at Colvestone because I was surrounded by grown men – and it was a place where everybody had something to prove.

It was only a short walk through streets I knew well, and over the years I walked it thousands of times. I had a job painting and decorating with Islington council. It was a decent job and I was working with a good group of men. Each night I would leave the flat and weave my way up and down the local streets with my bag packed to bursting with my protector, my gloves and my training clothes. I walked the same streets coming back from friends' homes, and later in life, when I quit the painting game, I never got lost when I turned to mini-cab driving.

Inside the gym were some great fighters. The first day I walked through the door I immediately saw former British champion Kirkland Laing and future triple world champion Dennis Andries. I had seen the two fighters before at shows, especially at York Hall in Bethnal Green, but at Colvestone they were at work and it was different. There were others that I recognised and there were some that recognised me. Anybody that has taken part in competitive sport will understand the sensation I felt when I walked through the door, but in most sports that feeling of uncertainty and excitement is restricted to match day. At my new gym, every night from 7 p.m. was match day.

Colvestone was not a gym for the squeamish, and from my first visit I realised that it was not a place for play. I was there because I was hungry to be a successful fighter, and it was a hunger that every man and boy there shared. I had my boxing dreams, just like all the boxers I saw on that first visit, and there was no way that I was going to be intimidated by a few hard stares. I could fight, and I had to prove it that first day in the ring at Colvestone. I survived the first session and gradually I won them all over.

There was one particular fighter at Colvestone who proved difficult to win over, and that was because he was the golden boy when I arrived. His name was Darren Dyer, and before I switched clubs I had seen him on the circuit and knew that he had won two national junior championships. He was about a year younger than I was, but he always seemed to me like he wanted to prove something whenever we sparred. I eventually became the top amateur at Colvestone and I don't think Darren was ever happy with that. But the ferocious sparring never stopped us becoming friends. He has always been there for me over the years, and I was at Wembley in 1986 when he finally won the Amateur Boxing Association welterweight title.

I believed that at Colvestone there was the drive and the talent to make anything possible, and that included winning the Olympics and a world title. All fighters like to dream, and at

Colvestone I knew the dreams had far more chance of becoming reality because each session was a struggle. I would arrive with a fire in my belly – it was, to me, real boxing and I loved every second of it.

The gym was run by Harry Griver and he was a great character in boxing. He drove a London taxi during the day and spent his evenings coaching at the gym. He put every single part of his body and soul into running that club. He was also a rebel and had a justifiable reputation for upsetting people. Even at the gym his eccentric behaviour was legendary, but his commitment was never questioned.

At Colvestone there were always different fighters coming through the door for sparring sessions. Some were pros, others were amateurs, but the place started to get a reputation as the hardest gym in London and possibly the country. It helped that Dennis Andries was a regular, because he was without doubt one of boxing's toughest and roughest men.

I have never sparred with anybody that was stronger than Dennis. By the time I arrived at Colvestone there was already a deep respect for him in the gym because he had been a pro for five years. He was a huge presence on the boxing scene and we kind of developed together at Colvestone. I think Dennis groomed me during the years we spent together.

Kirkland Laing was another sparring partner. He is arguably the best British fighter never to have won a world title and I am sad that he never fulfilled his potential. I have never seen a more naturally blessed fighter than Kirk, and sparring with him was both a learning experience and a frustrating lesson. He could move each way and counter with both hands from seemingly impossible angles.

In 1982, the year that I went to Colvestone, Kirk had a fight in America, in Detroit, with Panama's feared Roberto Duran. I had helped Kirk prepare and I was looking forward to the fight because it was between one of my idols and my sparring friend. The fight was a surprise victory for Kirk. He was gifted, but I didn't expect him to pull it off against a superfighting legend. But he cracked it and became an even greater inspiration to us, not just at Colvestone, but to boxers everywhere.

I was a new Michael Watson when I entered the National Amateur Boxing Club championships in November 1983. I was eighteen, strong, and after a year at Colvestone I knew I was on a roll. I won the London title and in January 1984 I finally won a national title when I beat Graeme Hall of Whitburn at the Grosvenor House for the NABC Class C under-75 kilo championship. The final, like so many in amateur boxing, was a bit messy, but when it was over I had the title and just a few weeks to prepare before the start of the senior Amateur Boxing Association championships. It was also Olympic year, and I started to think very seriously about being in the British team for the Los Angeles games.

During the summer of 1983 I had formed a strong relationship with Eric Seccombe at Colvestone. He helped me a lot because he was a calm man with a good boxing brain. He slowed me down, made me think more, and that helped me relax in the ring. Eric stayed with me up until the final months of my career nearly ten years later.

Eric had a red taxi and I can remember sitting in it and talking outside my mum's flat after he had driven me home. We developed a strong bond, and in boxing that is essential because a fighter needs to be able to trust his trainer and have faith in him. At that time I believed one hundred per cent in Eric and his ability to help me realise my dream of getting to the Olympics.

The days dragged by in the build-up to the start of the London ABAs which I had to win before moving forward to the national stages. It might seem a bit insignificant now, but in the cold January and February of 1984 my whole life was devoted to winning the north-east London divisional championship at York Hall on the first of March. The ABA championships, especially at local level, are all that matter to a young fighter, and the day I walked into York Hall for my big test it felt like I had arrived in the real world of boxing.

In the final at middleweight I had to beat local boxer Harry Lawson from the Repton club. Lawson had won a few junior titles but I knew I would be too slick and powerful for him. I won when he was cut above the eye in Round Two and the fight was stopped, but it was not as easy as I thought it would be. I had two weeks after that win to get ready for the semi-finals back at York Hall and a possible confrontation with England's number one, John Beckles. It was only after beating Lawson that I realised how excited I was about possibly fighting Beckles. It kept me awake at night and at one point I thought I would have to get up and shadow-box to calm down. I know of fighters that have to go for runs or get in a gym for an hour after winning fights because they need to stop the adrenalin pumping.

In the gym Harry and Eric put their heads together to come up with ways to beat Beckles. We had all dismissed the two other fighters in the semi-final draw. A few days before I beat Lawson I had gone with Harry in his cab to Tottenham town hall to watch Beckles win the north-west London title. He was powerful and he could clearly bang, but he was slow and I knew that I was much faster than he was. There was an added edge to the upcoming and inevitable rivalry because Beckles boxed for the Islington club and I lived in Islington.

On the day of the London semi-finals at York Hall on 15 March 1984 I followed my usual routine. I woke late, had a light breakfast and waited for Eric to pick me up at the flat. The weigh-in for the fights took place in the afternoon on the stage at the old hall. I was comfortable at middleweight limit and felt relaxed. Eric was there, and Harry, and one or two from the gym were hanging about. Beckles was also there and he made the weight but I noticed that he looked drained. There was a pale sheen to his skin and I knew that meant he was weak at the weight.

Next we had to wait for the draw to take place. We sat in the seats and talked and just tried to keep the atmosphere nice and calm. The draw was slow. There was a problem with the light-weights and it needed to be drawn again, and the officials on the stage were arguing. Harry was laughing at their behaviour and then we heard one of them say 'Middleweights'. We all stopped talking and focused on the man with his hand in a small sack.

'Watson, Colvestone . . .' His voice trailed away as he looked up with the second name in his hand.

I knew then.

'Beckles, Islington.'

I had the fight I wanted.

A few minutes later I was on my way back to Mum's dinner table and a meal. It was to be the first of many big fights in my life, but at that time there was no bigger fight on the amateur circuit in London. When Eric left, I could sense that he was just a bit nervous so I followed him outside and told him to relax.

After I had eaten I went up to my bedroom and put my head down for a few hours. I didn't sleep but I relaxed, and that was all that I needed. Eric came to get me at about five p.m. and we drove the few miles to York Hall. I remember it was dark and cold when he dropped me off.

It was early and the boxing had only just started, but already there was a big crowd inside and a tremendous buzz. I started to walk to the back of the hall but I was stopped by a lot of people I knew or had previously met. I quickly realised that my fight was the centre of attention, and by the time I found my way to the small changing room up behind the stage I was ready to go out and fight. Eric and Harry settled me down and then the visitors started to arrive. This was, I imagined, what it was like in the big-time. I was full of energy. I just wanted to get in the ring and show what I could do, and do it in the least amount of time possible.

Darren showed up and confirmed what I had been thinking. 'The place is banged, there's not a ticket left,' he told us.

Many years later an ABA official came up to me at a pro show and told me that in thirty years of involvement he had never known a night like the one when I met Beckles.

In the changing room I started to get ready slowly and carefully. Eric and Harry seemed surprised at how calm I was, but they needn't have been. It was my first real test and I was desperate to get out there and prove that I was a real fighter. I have always known my true potential and I felt confident.

Ten minutes before I was due in the ring I was called out to the gloving-up table to get my gloves laced and secured by the ABA's officials. At this point a fighter often gets to look at his opponent, but Beckles was not there. I went back with my gloves on and hit Eric's hands with a few light hooks to keep warm and see how the gloves felt. Harry showed up again to make sure I was calm. A few minutes later an ABA official came to the door and shouted, 'Watson, one minute.' It was time.

I walked from the changing room and through the door to the stage, and all I could see was the empty ring and hundreds and hundreds of people. I went down the few steps and then I was at the back of the hall. There are no security guards in amateur boxing and at first I could not see a way for me to get to the ring. I looked up and saw Beckles climb in. He looked big under the lights. I carried on walking and the people just seemed to part, while the noise kept getting louder and louder.

I reached the ring and Eric stood back to allow me up first. I ducked under the top rope and looked over at Beckles as I stood up. He had taken his robe off. I could see that he was extremely powerful, and I knew then that if I messed about he was going to knock me out. He had a knockout punch in his right cross and his left hook. He was more mature than me at about twenty-one, and finally I could see why people were nervous about me fighting him. I was the underdog – and I was loving every second of it.

Harry backed away to stand with a group of friends, his regular boxing pals. Some of them doubted his wisdom, but he told them to stop worrying.

'Beckles is dead at the weight and this kid can fight. Trust me,' he told them.

We were brought together in the middle of the ring by the referee to touch gloves and then I went back to the corner and Eric put my gumshield in.

'Good luck, son,' he told me.

I looked out over the crowd in the final seconds before the opening bell because I wanted to enjoy every moment. People were standing and shouting under the thick layer of smoke and I can clearly remember thinking, in the few seconds before the fight started, that this was what it was all about. I loved the attention and the excitement, the thrill of suspense and putting the crowd on the edge of their seats, the anticipation of overcoming the odds. That was my motivation. I was powered by my self-belief and determination. The will to win spurred me on. The same will would help me many years later.

Beckles never stood a chance. My punches connected with his chin, and then I felt his legs go, and then his whole body was gone. He was trapped in the corner trying to defend himself, and there was nothing he could do. A final left hook finished it, and when the referee stepped in to save poor John Beckles, less than a minute had gone in Round One. York Hall was a scene of mayhem.

I had won, and moved closer to the Olympics. Also, it was my nineteenth birthday.

Chapter 3

The win against John Beckles changed the way I looked at boxing. Before that night I was serious, but after that short and explosive fight I realised that I really did have a future in the ring. I think a lot of people came to the same conclusion.

There was barely time for me to enjoy the glory before I had to get back in the ring, and this time the venue was the beautiful Royal Albert Hall and the occasion was the London finals. I had an easy win against Lenny Thorne from the Fisher club in South London. He had seen the Beckles fight and he ran all night.

Away from the ring I was picking up a following and starting to get a lot of compliments in the community. Mum was always proud of what I achieved in my early amateur career, but now other people, some strangers, complimented her on my win.

The win had a downside, however. At Colvestone shortly after I won the London title Dennis Andries grabbed me for a private word. He had a concerned look on his face.

'Mike,' he told me, 'watch for the sharks now. Watch for them all.'

That was all he said, but I knew what he meant because I had been approached by a lot of people since the shock win over Beckles. It was to be the start of the endless promises that I would keep on hearing right up until my last fight. I have always respected Dennis and believe that he is one of the most underrated fighters in British boxing history.

Two weeks after the London finals I went to Gloucester for the English quarter-finals. I met an old opponent there, Graeme Hall, and moved closer to the Olympics when I knocked him out in the first round. Three months earlier I had beaten him on points to win the NABA Class C title. The journey back from Gloucester in the back of Eric's red cab was full of hope. In a four-month period I had won a national title, beaten the best middleweight in Britain in less than a minute and was just two fights away from an Olympic place.

After the win at Gloucester I was introduced to various men on the fringes of the boxing circuit. Some claimed to have the ear of certain promoters, and they all spoke boldly of great wealth and success, but none of them did anything other than speak. In the boxing business talk is cheap and I heard a lot of cheap talk.

The day finally came when I had to go with Harry and Eric to Preston for the British semi-finals, and what I considered to be the semi-final for the middleweight position at the Olympics. In my mind I was on that plane heading for Los Angeles long before we climbed into Eric's red cab for the long journey north.

It was an early meet for the drive and it was clear that it would be a long day. After nearly five hours we arrived at the Guildhall in Preston for the weigh-in, and instantly I had a feeling that there was something wrong. The semi-final stage of the ABA championships involves the champion of Wales and Scotland and the best two in England. The names go in a hat and the two English boxers are kept apart. The other English boxer was Brian Schumacher, who was originally from Liverpool but was boxing for the Navy, and I could tell from the weigh-in that he was not certain about beating me from the way he looked over and nodded when we were waiting to get on the scales.

I could not quite put my finger on what was wrong and both Eric and Harry told me to relax and not to worry, but I couldn't, and eventually I worked out what it was that was making me feel a bit uneasy. I feared that the Scottish and Welsh officials did not like the English ones and that that could lead to bad blood. A few years later, the Welsh and Scottish associations broke away; from that point on the ABA championships have never carried the same weight.

I was not scared of losing because I honestly believed that I was the best amateur middleweight in the country and that I would knock out anybody put in front of me. But I had seen bad decisions at local level, and Harry had a long list of atrocities that he would recite whenever anybody provoked him. He had lost a lot of good fighters to the street after bad decisions, and that was something that particularly annoyed him.

At the draw my name was read out next to Scotland's Russell Barker. I knew absolutely nothing about him other than the fact that his club was in Dundee. We left the Guildhall and found somewhere to eat.

It was a long and slow afternoon and the waiting game was to continue because I was not boxing until late into the night. By the time I got in the ring I felt like I had lost a bit of freshness, but none of my confidence.

The fight was not much of a spectacle but I was sure I had won clearly, and when it was over both Eric in the corner and Harry, who was down by the steps at the bottom of the ring, congratulated me. I was not a hundred per cent happy because I knew I had tried too hard for a knock out and neglected my jab and basic punches. Still, I knew I had done more than enough. In the back of my mind, though, I was still conscious of the uneasy feeling I had had when we had arrived that morning.

The referee called the pair of us into the middle of the ring at the end of the contest, and as I stood there with my wrist in his hand I started to have a sinking feeling in my heart. The ring announcer faced us and read out the decision, and even before the words filled his mouth I knew that the Olympic dream was over. The winner would go to Wembley for the final and a direct box-off for the Olympic place. The loser would leave Preston with nothing, not even a medal or a basic trophy.

'The winner on points and 1984 ABA middleweight finalist is . . . Barker.'

I dropped my head in disbelief. I could hear Harry's outraged shouting. He was just particularly upset because seeing how far I had come he knew how far I could go. He also liked me because I was honest and straight with him at all times. He would always tell people that I was a 'good boy'.

'Forget it, Mike,' Eric said when I finally walked back to the corner.

I would forget it in time, but it wasn't easy. It was a complete joke, and it can still make me very angry now. I found out some details after the fight that helped me make up mind about my future. It was probably just a coincidence, but I don't think so, and I felt I was robbed in Preston.

The drive home was long and boring. Nobody had anything to say after the inevitable rants from both Eric and Harry, which had dried up by the time we were on the outskirts of town. Harry was always very colourful with his descriptions of people that were on his wrong side, so listening to him was often amusing – but not that night. The back of the cab was dark and silent by the time we had reached the motorway and I finally had some time to think.

I had just one thought on my mind. It never took me very long to make a decision.

'I'm going pro,' I announced.

Nobody reacted to my comment so I said it again.

'That's good, son,' said Eric.

'Yeah, that's good, boy. We'll talk about it tomorrow,' added Harry.

I had heard all of the arguments that agents of the professional promoters put forward about fighting for money, and how it was a waste to stay amateur, but I had dismissed them all up until that evening. I reasoned that I was the one getting up in the ring and doing the fighting, that it was my right to choose and I had picked the Olympics. In Preston that dream died, and I knew it was time to quit the amateurs, find a manager, a promoter and a trainer and turn professional.

'Yeah, let's talk in the morning,' I replied.

Ten minutes later I fell asleep and only woke up when the cab lurched to a noisy stop outside the flats about four hours later.

The next morning I told Mum and she nodded and said she would discuss it with Uncle Joe. I have no idea if she ever spoke to my dad. I never did. I saw him after the loss and told him what had happened, and then he went off to work like always. A few nights later Uncle Joe came to eat with Mum, Jeff and me and we had a chat about turning professional. It was settled that I would.

Mum and Uncle Joe agreed with me that Eric should apply for a licence and become my trainer. Mum always liked Eric and liked the fact that he treated me like his own son. We did have a very strong relationship.

So I asked Eric if he would be my trainer and he said yes, which meant I just had to find a promoter and a manager. I was not going to be suckered by one of the men who had been whispering down my ear and promising the earth since the night I stopped Beckles. I needed a real manager and promoter, and I picked the best in the country at that time: Mickey Duff.

I knew that Duff had been interested in me from conversations with different people, and when I mentioned Duff's name to Harry he said it would be easy to set up a meeting. It was, and about ten days after losing in Preston a meeting was arranged at Duff's offices in Wardour Street.

At that time Duff had five or six British champions and had been looking after fighters for about twenty-five years. He had promoted or managed world champions and had a long-established deal to screen boxing on the BBC. He was by far the most powerful man in British boxing in May 1984 when I arranged to see him.

I took Mum and Uncle Joe. We entered Duff's office and he was all smiles and handshakes and compliments. After a few minutes of pleasantries Duff got straight to the business end of the meeting. I listened, taking it all in and adding up the money in my head. Uncle Joe asked a few questions and Duff answered.

Duff went through lists of all the fighters he had made champions of Britain or the world, and all the fighters he had made rich over the years. His record at that time was close to perfect. Very few fighters had fallen out with him or voiced any serious concerns about his dual role as manager and promoter. The three of us sat there and his words seemed to make more and more sense.

I would win the Southern Area belt, the British title, the European title and then follow Jim Watt, John H. Stracey, Maurice Hope and Charlie Magri to a world title fight. All I had to do was listen to Duff, keep winning, and in about eight years' time I would be able to retire with a fat bank account.

As the meeting drifted on I was starting to feel more special and talented than ever. He told me that he would make me a champion. This was his bait to draw me in, and it worked.

He asked Mum about my weight, my eating habits and whether I had a girlfriend. She told him the truth and that seemed to satisfy him. At that time – I was only nineteen – I could make the middleweight limit easily, and I had a good diet. I did have a girlfriend called Zara, whose family were from Morocco. The relationship was good, but I was very focused on my career as I was determined to reach the top. And I believed that, with Duff's help, I could get there.

After signing a contract with Duff, the licence arrived from the British Boxing Board of Control and I was officially a professional. I had taken all of their required medical examinations and paid the small fee, and by the end of the summer of 1984 I was waiting for Mickey Duff to come up with a fight.

My life went on in the same way. I got up each day to go to work, came home quickly and then met Eric at Colvestone to train. In the gym there was absolutely no difference in the sparring or the way I looked at the sport.

I knew that the slower pace of boxing as a professional would suit me a lot better, and so did Duff, Eric and Harry. I enjoyed having the extra time in the ring that I would have as a pro. I would be doing three-minute rounds, but there would be six of them, or even eight during my first year. I had started to slow down long before I went pro and that had been the problem in my last fight as an amateur.

By September I was ready to fight, and a name, a date and a venue for my debut were finally given to Eric and me. It meant nothing to me, but Harry and Eric had a few words about the choice that Duff had put forward.

I was due to fight Winston Wray at the Royal Albert Hall on 16 October over six three-minute rounds. I knew nothing about Wray, but Harry had his sources and got to work finding out as much as he could. Wray was from Manchester and had been a former north-west counties amateur champion at light heavy-weight. He was only a few years older at twenty-three, and taller than I was, but certainly not what is known in boxing as a 'body'. He had lost five but won seven, and had never been matched in an easy fight. Looking back it is hard to imagine any so-called prospect today having such a difficult first fight. But it was to get even harder for me.

When I returned to the Royal Albert Hall as a professional it was a very different atmosphere. The amateur game is relaxed and people know each other and take time to speak, but most pros are just there to get in the ring, get out and get away. I was excited by the prospect of fighting in front of a big crowd on a big night, but Eric and Harry both seemed a bit low-key. I told them the same thing that I had told them a few months earlier when I met John Beckles at York Hall: relax.

As the fight approached I was increasingly calm. It showed in the ring – I stopped Wray in four rounds. I could hear the cheering, especially from Mum and members of the Evering Pentecostal church. I enjoyed every second of the fight and it was a lot easier than I had expected. Wray was slower than anybody I had ever met, and I was able to pick him off with ease with shots from either hand. He was on his feet, but he was unable to defend himself when the referee moved forward. My first fight was over and it was time for a little celebrating.

After my first win as a professional I had to wait over four months for my next outing. I fought a quality and ultimately tragic man called Johnny Elliot. The fight was over eight rounds at York Hall, and thankfully I stopped him in the eighth and last round. I knocked him down four times in total but he was a good fighter, very proud, and he kept getting up and coming back at me.

I fought three more times in 1985 and stopped all three opponents. Dennis Sheehan went in three and was on the canvas once, Gary Tomlinson was dropped twice and stopped in Round Four, and in November, former dangerman Martin McEwan survived to Round Six before he was rescued by the referee. McEwan was also knocked down and it was obvious to the knowledgeable that I was developing nicely and that I had a very good punch in my right hand.

Away from the ring I was seeing Zara, but I was still living at home. I needed to be quite independent so I could concentrate on my boxing.

The fights continued in 1986, and in February I sent Tooting's Karl Barwise tumbling in three at the Royal Albert Hall. I was unbeaten in six, and all of my opponents had failed to hear the final bell. Then Eric was told I would be fighting Carlton Warren at the Royal Albert Hall on 7 May, just a few weeks after my twenty-first birthday.

Carlton was a nice man, but I knew I had to fear him in the ring. He had an unbeaten record of three and had knocked out all three of his opponents. I knew that the fight would be a test – two fighters with a future in a fight to decide who was going to go forward and who was going to go backwards. At the Royal Albert Hall that night my whole career was at stake.

We made a little bit of boxing history that night. The fight was savage and we both fought like we had nowhere else to go, because that is exactly where the loser was going. Warren took some tremendous punches but he kept coming back. He caught me and hurt me several times, but I rocked him back so often that I was convinced he would go. He never did, but at the end of six furious rounds the referee raised my hand. I was seven and zero and my career was on track.

I walked back to the corner and something hit my leg and then something else hit my boot. I looked down and saw coins on the canvas. Loads and loads of coins and they kept on coming. I had never seen it before but I knew what it was – in boxing they call it nobbins, and that night was the last time it happened at a fight at the Royal Albert Hall, one of British boxing's most sacred venues. The tradition calls for the two fighters to remain in the ring and applaud the crowd's applause and then, when the coins and cheers have faded, the fighters get to split the spoils. I felt I'd earned every extra penny in what was the toughest fight of my life so far.

I had been a professional boxer for nineteen months and had fought seven times at regular intervals of two to three months. So I was surprised when I was told the day after beating Warren that I was boxing again in just thirteen days and that I was due to meet James Cook over eight rounds. Cook was a quality fighter, and late in his career he won both the British and European titles and remains in the business to this day as a very highly respected trainer.

The fight against Cook saved my boxing life. At that stage I honestly could not see a way I could lose. The six-rounder with Carlton sent a warning to my brain, but I wasn't listening. When I got in the ring with Cook I was too confident, and for a boxer overconfidence is one of his most dangerous enemies. Cook beat me on points that night, which gave me the wake-up call I needed at the right time. The fight was just an eight-round learning fight and not really important in the grand scheme of things, but to me it was the most important fight of my career and I learned the most important lesson. I would never ever underestimate an opponent again or cut any corners. So in a way the defeat was the biggest victory so far.

I did ask myself why Duff had pitched me into two such difficult fights in such a short space of time, but I guess that he just wanted to know if I could really fight. The defeat was good for me, and Duff knew it. I think he was just testing me before he invested any more time and energy on my career. He was a hard boxing man and a firm businessman.

I was out on the road running five miles less than twelve hours after losing to Cook. I was determined to make that loss the turning point in my life.

The loss put a tiny dent in my confidence as a fighter and I needed a win to get it back. It also put a halt to the long line of new friends that were increasingly starting to attach themselves to me, and that was good news. There was a time when it was just Eric and Harry at my side, but that had changed and more people had started to come to the fights with me. When James Cook's hand was raised, most of the new friends faded into the background.

I was starting to spend more and more time with Zara and I found the comfort I got from the relationship very reassuring. I had neglected a lot of things during the six years that I had been boxing, and in the weeks and months after the Cook loss I started to take a good look at my surroundings and the way I treated people. Boxing had become my entire life and nothing else had mattered, but now I realised that I needed close friends, loved ones and family. The defeat was not only the catalyst for me to alter the course of my boxing career, but it also set me on a better path as a human being. I had been selfish in pursuit of success, the loss made me realise that there was more to life than boxing. It also made me realise that I was not yet the finished article that I had come to believe I was.

July 1986 was a great month for me. I stepped back in the ring and knocked out Simon Collins at Wembley Stadium. This restored some of my pride, and the news that Zara gave me one night at the end of July lifted my spirits even higher. I was going to be a father, and that was the final motivation I needed to go to the very top in my chosen profession.

Zara and I were happy and I was spending more time with her. Now that I was earning money as a fighter I had quit the painting business, bought myself a nice car and was working for a mini-cab firm in Islington. The change of job gave me far more time for training and relaxing. It also gave me, I reasoned, more time to be a father when my first child was born.

At the end of 1986 I had a perfect workout against one of the sport's most durable men when I went eight rounds with Alan Baptiste at Wembley Arena. I won clearly and had Baptiste over from a short right cross, but the most important thing was that I had gone eight rounds and looked good going the distance. After the fight I settled down for a nice Christmas and a new year that I knew would bring change in my life on both sides of the ropes.

Zara gave me a beautiful daughter on 20 March 1987. We named her Jamilla Mary Watson and I was an instant and doting father. I could not quite comprehend that this little beautiful bundle was my child. She was too much, too lovely.

The first three months of 1987 were the busiest of my life. I stopped Ian Chantler in early January and beat Ralph Smiley over eight rounds in February. The night before Jamilla was born I won again when I was pushed the full eight-round margin by Cliff Gilpin. After that I had a break of over six months to come to terms with being a father.

I know I was a good father at the time because I know how much love I felt for my little daughter. I would spend days just holding and feeding her, and I could see that my mum was very proud.

Come the end of the summer Duff was starting to tell me about fights he had planned, the route he wanted to take and the title he wanted me to win. He was a traditional man and wanted to get me a leading position for one of the two middleweight titles, and then I would be able to force a fight with the champion. I stepped back in the ring in October 1987 and won twice, but away from the ring there was another quite serious development: Zara was pregnant again and the baby was due the following February. The issue of marriage came up, but we knew that there would be problems we could not overcome, the main one being religion.

October was also the month that my dad finally did what he had wanted to do for twenty-five years. He packed his bags, said goodbye and returned to Jamaica. He had always talked about Jamaica and there were a lot of times when it was annoying. He would insist there was no place like home and just go on and on. He was never a bad man, but he was never much of a father. Increasingly Uncle Joe had taken on that role.

My dad had a son in Manchester, Jamaica, and his name was Derek, and the older I got the more he talked about his other son. It would drive me mad at times having to listen to him talking about his other son and his life in Jamaica before he arrived in London. My dad had never shown a great interest in my boxing, even when I was a youngster at Crown and Manor. He only came to one of my fights, preferring to stay at the flat with Jeff when I boxed.

He had told Mum that he was going back for a holiday and asked if we all wanted to go. Mum said no. She knew he was not coming back. She knew that once he walked out the door she would never see him again. I knew it too, and I'm sure Jeff did, but it was not something that we all sat around talking about.

It was probably as much a relief for him as it was for us. It does seem odd when I look back on it, but at the time there was nothing unusual about it. One day he was there at the flat and we said hello as usual and then he went back to silently watching the TV. (I was staying most nights with Zara and Jamilla at the time). I went back the following day and Mum told me that he had gone. I never saw him again. He saw me, years later, but I was in a coma. A tabloid paper had found him and flew him over. He visited me and touched my hand and my head. Mum saw him then but she had nothing to say to him. A few years ago I saw a picture of him in one of the newspaper cuttings from the time when I was in hospital. I didn't miss him because I never really got to know him.

In 1988 Duff decided that I would fight Americans and get some valuable experience against men who are known in the boxing business as journeymen. They come to fight, bringing experience and durability, but they are not meant to win. It is the tried and tested way for young prospects to gain the knowledge they will need in major fights. I tore through the American imports with a fury that shocked a lot of people.

Typically, Duff matched me with Dangerous Don Lee, who was one of the most avoided and feared middleweights from that period. Lee was no longer the dangerman he had been in the mid-eighties, but he was still a considerable step up in class for me when we met at the Wembley Arena in February 1988. The fight was savage at times and Lee could really bang hard, but I started to get to him and in Round Five the referee called a halt to the fight. Lee's lip was badly cut and I was ready to set him up for a painful end. It was the best win on my record and the first against a real world-class fighter. Six days after beating Lee I became a father for the second time when Zara gave birth to Layla Ezra Watson. I was twenty-two.

I fought in March, April, May, July and October. I met a succession of America's top losers and added my name to the list of men that had previously stopped or knocked them out. I was getting a reputation and finally gaining some international recognition. I quit the mini-cab profession simply because the boxing was becoming more lucrative.

One of the quick wins in 1988 was in Las Vegas in July. The result in my record reads technical draw. However, I was taking Israel Cole apart when he suffered a cut above his left eye and under Nevada rules the fight was stopped and the drawn verdict announced. The fight took place at Caesar's Palace and was a great experience for me. I believed that I would be back one day involved in my own superfight at Caesar's, just like all the ring legends of the seventies and eighties.

By now my relationship with Zara was coming to an end. Once again boxing was starting to take complete control of my life. By the start of 1989 I had a world ranking from the WBA and I had begun to take more notice of the domestic scene. At that time the number one middleweight attraction in Britain was East London's Nigel Benn.

In 1988 Benn had won the Commonwealth middleweight title. He was a dangerous fighter because of his punching power. I had watched him a few times on TV and was impressed with his power – he could take a man out with just one punch – but I saw tiny flaws and knew that I could exploit the gaps.

Mickey Duff reluctantly agreed a fight between us. He had doubts about whether I could beat him. When I talked to Eric about it he also seemed to think it would be a very hard fight. It made me curious that the two people in charge of my boxing career were not keen for me to share a ring with Benn, and it made me absolutely determined to prove them wrong.

In January and March of 1989 Duff let me loose on two more Americans at the Royal Albert Hall and I beat the pair of them in three rounds. Just a few days before the fight in March against Franklin Owens I told some reporters that I would beat Benn because of my superior boxing skills, though I knew deep inside that it would not be easy. When I was asked how I would deal with his power, I laughed and said, 'No problem.' I just believed that I would beat him. I knew it would not go the distance and that I would knock him out.

I had never seen Nigel fight in the flesh, but I had watched him defend his title on TV, and I wanted the chance to take it from him. I was fed up with people underestimating me, and also with the surrounding negative publicity, which, in part, was coming from Benn's camp. I knew I could take control in the ring.

Chapter 4

Benn was intimidating inside the ring. He had a lethal punch that was capable of destroying his opponents. He also had a good publicity machine behind him. I didn't like Benn much then. He was loud and saying negative things about me. The way he tried to belittle me really annoyed me. But it was all part of the hype to create animosity between us and it worked! The build up to the fight guaranteed that it would be explosive and unforgettable. My record was much better than Nigel's record. I had lost just once, and there was the draw with Israel Cole in Las Vegas, but I had also stopped or knocked out seventeen men in twenty-one wins. My statistics were also better because I had met much tougher and far more seasoned fighters, but I was sensible enough to realise that he was a star and I was just the nice guy. The hard, 'bad boy' image kept him in the papers and this image became the main theme for our fight. It was bad versus good and it immediately caught on as an idea, mainly because neither of us had to do much acting. I was even portrayed in print as a mummy's boy who was not afraid to get my hands dirty during a little spring cleaning. I think my local paper in Islington called me the 'Smooth Mover with a Hoover'. Nigel was the 'Dark Destroyer'.

By late March, about twenty days after I had beaten Franklin Owens at the Royal Albert Hall, there was no sign of the fight becoming a reality. I had heard the rumours and the figures, but nobody had actually sat down and discussed a fight between Nigel and me. A meeting was set to discuss it, and when Duff called to tell me that he had a contract for me, a big smile broke out on my face. I told Mum and Jeffrey the good news. Jeffrey went to fetch Lennard, and when he came into the room, Mum showed him a headline that read: Watson set to fight Benn. Lennard later gave me some good advice. He told me that I was now going to be in the media spotlight and that I should always be truthful and keep a cool head, so that even in defeat I would always have respect. I've never forgotten his words. I heard that the date was set for 21 May and that there was a plan to pitch a tent in Finsbury Park. The same night that I heard this piece of news I went with Eric in his cab to have a look at the park. It was less than two miles from my mum's place, so the journey was quick and short. As dusk settled I walked with Eric on the football pitches that were still there even though the Saturday and Sunday leagues had finished for the season. I could feel a buzz from just being at the site, even if there were still about eight weeks to go. Nobody in Finsbury Park recognised me that night, but I knew it would be different after the fight.

Six weeks before the fight I moved out to a friend of Eric's in Enfield. His name was Terry Brady and he had enough room in his house for us to stay and create a training camp. At Terry's house both Eric and I could get our heads and our preparation perfect. Moving to Terry's place was a good idea because life at home with Mum and my other life with Zara and my daughters was too much for me to deal with in the weeks before the fight.

Inevitably, my relationship with Zara had suffered because of my concentration on my career and we had actually split. The training and the fight allowed me to put my absent daughters out of my mind for a few weeks but there were a lot of nights in Enfield when I prayed in silence for both of them.

Each day, as the night in the tent slowly approached, I was finding out just how lonely a boxer in a major fight can become. I had Eric, and Terry was a terrific man, but I had moved away from a lot of the people I had spent most days with during the last few years. I was lonely, and that left me with a lot of time for private prayer and mental preparation, which I certainly needed for what was the most important fight of my life. In the middle of the long nights when I was praying and relaxing I devised a plan to beat Nigel. I felt bold a long time before the fight, and Eric and Duff were nervous that I had peaked too early, but I was in control because my head was right. Simple prayer had given me strength, and for several weeks I knew the fight was won, the victory secure and that my life was about to change.

I would occasionally go back to Mum's for a meal or just for a change of scenery, and about two weeks before the fight I was sitting quietly at her table reading through a few papers. There seemed to be coverage somewhere every day and I think I was reading about Nigel's next fight, the one after me, which was due to be against either Tommy Hearns or Roberto Duran or even Sugar Ray Leonard.

The final ten days before the fight were uneventful. The papers, as usual, were full of the fight and on the day, as I relaxed at Terry's house, I even saw news bulletins about it. I drove down with Eric to Finsbury Park through familiar territory. It was a simple journey and when I got there I just stood and took in the whole scene, which looked particularly strange because it was a place I knew but it had been transformed. I can remember seeing a helicopter flying over the park and thinking that I was in the middle of a big event, an event that would forever show up in the boxing record books.

I had been at the tent the previous day and what had struck me most was the smell of damp. During my visit Ambrose had taken me to one side to advise me to do a practice walk from my changing room to the ring. He was concerned about the noise on fight night and he didn't want me to panic and forget which way to walk. Duff had seen him talking to me and sent across one of his men to grab me away. Ambrose also told me that it would take Nigel more than two minutes to get to the ring and that he was warning me against Duff doing something stupid. Duff had previously said that if Nigel took more than two minutes to reach the ring, we would all climb out and go back to the changing room. It never bothered me because I knew I was going to be standing there in front of five thousand people and loving every second of it. It was just another example of Duff losing his cool with Ambrose and not being able to see that it was a wind-up, an easy way to undermine Duff.

There were times when I could hardly recognise Duff as the man I had agreed terms with in 1984. Back then he was at the top of the boxing pile and nobody had put one over on him in twenty-odd years, but by the time of my fight with Nigel in 1989 I was no longer satisfied with the way he was managing my career. I felt that I was moving too fast for Duff, and I also got the idea that he truly believed that I would lose. He never told me before the fight, but I just knew. All fighters know when the men in charge of training, managing and promoting them think they will lose. Duff has always maintained that he was confident that I would win, and he insists he placed a huge bet on me to beat Benn. Eric knew I could win but even he had his doubts. Duff was convinced that I would lose and I know that for a fact, even if he claims the opposite.

We fought on a Sunday and on the day I was once again calm, in a little world of my own, and all I could hear from somewhere outside my changing room was the roar of thunder. I thought it was the weather and it took about an hour for me to accept it was the crowd. The atmosphere in the changing room

Aged seventeen, training at Colvestone gym

With Zara and our two daughters Jamilla and Layla

Jamilla and Layla, a few years later

With Mum, my constant support

With my brother Jeffrey, taking a break in Cornwall

Challenging Nigel Benn
for the Commonwealth
Middleweight
Championship in 1989

GETTY IMAGES

After this fight
I became known as
'The Force'

POPPERFOTO

Moments after becoming
Commonwealth
Middleweight Champion

Challenging Mike McCallum 'The Body Snatcher' for the WBA Middleweight Championship in 1990

GETTY IMAGES

Defending my Commonwealth Middleweight title against Craig Trotter

CLEVA

Still the Champion, after stopping Craig Trotter in the fifth round

POPPERFOTO

A boxer ...

WATSON

The
Force

... and a gentleman

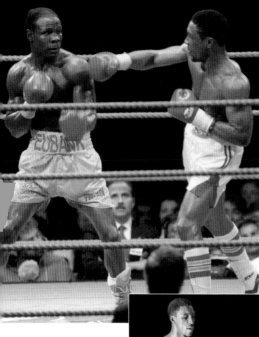

Challenging Chris Eubank
for the WBO Middleweight
Championship in 1991

Giving Chris a boxing lesson

aking it clear that
e split decision was
fair

COLOURSPORT

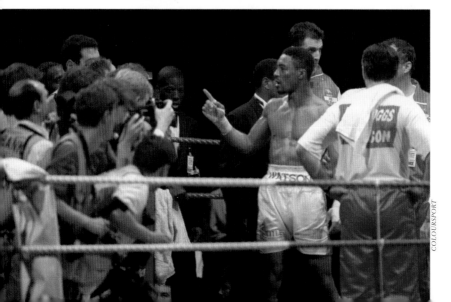

COLOURSPORT

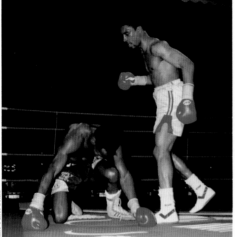

The rematch   The turning point

The moment one fight ended and another began

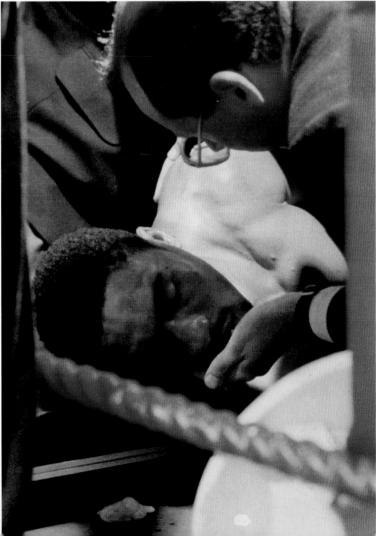

was growing more and more tense as the seconds ticked closer to the first bell. It was a great wait for a defining moment and one that I enjoyed immensely. A lot of the conversation revolved around the reports that Nigel had spent six hours or twelve hours on Friday night, depending on which paper you had read, getting his hair weaved and had apparently gone missing for most of the day before the fight. It was a mad story and one that made no sense. I believed that it was just the latest ruse from Nigel's spin masters and I dismissed it as another of their hoaxes, another exaggeration.

When the officials came to the room to put on the gloves there was an outburst from Duff because Ambrose had somehow managed to get elected as Nigel's representative. In important fights each boxer sends one of his team to witness the gloves being laced and taped in the opponent's changing room. It is a standard move and the unwritten rule is that the witness keeps his mouth shut and does not try to unnerve the opponent in any way. Ambrose was pleasant with me as always, but he could not keep quiet. Duff was screaming, and the inspector from the British Boxing Board of Control had no idea what to do. The gloves were eventually tightened, the room cleared and then we just had the short wait for the call to the ring. I stood up and I could feel the light shining on me and I knew I was blessed. I knew it was the night to show my gifts, to show what I had mastered.

The knock came, followed by the familiar call from the whip: 'Two minutes, Mike.'

I was ready and I set off for the walk from the back of the tent that I had rehearsed the previous day. My eyes immediately fixed on the neon light that highlighted the smoke swirling high above the four-roped arena, and all I could really sense was the feverish excitement, a mixture of heat and noise. I walked calmly through a tunnel of security guards inside a metal walkway, picking up words from the fans. Some were good and some were bad. It was an amazing experience to hear people shouting out my name and to hear people telling me that they loved me. It felt like I was stepping inside a film and not a tent on Finsbury Park – the colours and the faces gave it a look I had never known at a fight venue before. I reached the ringside and cleared the steps before pausing on the ring canvas, and then finally I eased myself through the ropes. The roar that lifted from the seats when my foot touched the canvas was the loudest I had ever heard at a fight.

I was looking out at the people and soaking it up when Nigel's music started. There was an Army band and behind them I could see Nigel in his glittering outfit with his fancy hair. We were all looking over at him and I could barely hear Duff when he turned to me.

'Don't worry, Mike,' he shouted.

'I'm not worried. It's only me and him in the ring,' I told him.

Nigel finally reached the ring and the noise level went up even higher. I was in my corner, loosely bouncing from foot to foot and just looking over at him without a trace of emotion on my face. I had no fear and I wanted Nigel to see that he was not under my skin in any way.

The ring started to clear and finally it was just the two of us and the third man, John Coyle, the referee. The fight was intense but that was not a shock, and he hit hard but that was not a shock either. I was the one who shocked everybody because I had come up with my own plan and it was based on the piece of genius that Muhammad Ali had used to defeat George Foreman in what was arguably his finest hour as a boxer. Ali was an old man when he travelled to Zaire in 1974 to try and regain the world heavyweight title. Nobody gave him a chance and most expected him to get knocked out quickly. Both Ali and I were massive underdogs against ferocious punchers. In Zaire, in the fight that is known as the Rumble in the Jungle, Ali perfected something that a lot of old timers used. He leaned back on the ropes with his guard high and his head out of reach. Ali called it Rope-A-Dope and it worked because in Round Eight he dropped an exhausted Foreman for the full count. Before the fight Ali had promised to move, and when he stood in front of Foreman in Round One and exchanged punches, 62,000 people fell silent. In Round Two Ali retreated to the ropes and the silence turned to screams of fear from Ali's men at ringside, but the Greatest knew what he was doing. He knew he had to test Foreman's will for a round before breaking his heart and spirit.

I also knew what I was doing. I stood with Nigel in Round One and landed with some heavy shots and took some heavy shots. It was a great round. At the bell I went back to the corner and the inevitable concerns and curses of Eric and Duff.

'Stop trading with him, move, move, move,' shouted Duff. His face was red, his voice hoarse from hollering at ringside.

I just nodded, rinsed my mouth out, took deep breaths and

prepared myself for the middle part of my strategy. In Round Two, just like Ali, I started to hold my hands very high and retreated to the ropes. I knew Nigel, just like Foreman, was not clever enough to pick holes in me. He was caught up in the hype surrounding his power and his future. In the ring I could feel his power and it was tremendous, but he was hitting me in the same places and at the same tempo. If he had used a better strategy he could have been a better fighter, but in my opinion he had put himself under too much pressure with the endless talk of knockouts and his thinking was clouded.

At the end of Round Four I knew the fight was over because at the bell he looked at me for a second and then gently tapped me. Nigel's fight was finished. His reign as Commonwealth middleweight champion was over, but I knew he wouldn't quit. I knew it would take a few more rounds to break him down and that was exactly what I was good at.

He took a slow beating for two more rounds and I watched as his face changed shape under the steady accuracy of my increasingly powerful punches. I was in a great position because I could take my time in the knowledge that my opponent could not hurt or beat me. I never abused the situation, and in Round Six Nigel turned away after I connected with my right on his eye. I stepped back, waiting for Mr Coyle to do his job and save him from further punishment. Nigel seemed to recover, nodded to the ref that he wanted to continue and then unleashed his final assault. I blocked the rush, and as he faltered and his mouth fell open in despair I fired out a left and he went over for the count. The last punch was a looping jab, not quite a hook, but at that stage he had nothing in the tank and the proverbial feather could have sent him tumbling. I felt for him when he landed on the canvas and I prayed that he would be fine. I remembered Lennard's words all those months earlier and I hope that I accepted the win with grace.

Duff and Eric were climbing all over me after the fight, but I was concerned for Nigel and tried to push them away. The ITV cameras were in the ring and Jim Rosenthal, one of broadcasting's true gentlemen, pulled us all to one side for an interview.

'You surprised a few people, Mike,' he said.

Before I could reply, Duff intercepted and blurted out, 'He surprised me.' It was the proof I needed that he had not fancied me from the very start.

Nigel was soon back on his feet and we were embracing. He took defeat better than he had taken winning and I know that losing to me made Nigel the fighter he went on to be. He admitted that his cause was lost early in the fight and that where I had a plan he had nothing more than a reputation. I ruined his reputation in the tent on Finsbury Park, but I launched my own.

Chapter 5

The day after beating Nigel Benn I saw my daughters and we sat on the floor playing at Mum's flat. They were growing up fast and I felt like I had not seen them for a long time, but really it was only a few weeks. Jamilla was two and two months and Layla was nearly eighteen months old.

Before I left Finsbury Park, Duff assured me that I would be at number one in the World Boxing Association's ratings, and that I would fight their champion Mike McCallum soon. I had no reason to doubt him.

I sat on the floor and the girls climbed over me and played with their toys. The TV was on in the background and I watched in shock as Nigel and Ambrose appeared on the sports news. It was like a bad dream. I had beaten him soundly in six rounds less than twenty-four hours earlier and I had hoped that that would put an end to the publicity he had been receiving. I was wrong. I sat with my mouth open listening to excuses and then hearing his plans. He was going to America, he was going to win a world title and then he would come back and fight me. He actually said that he would return with a world championship belt and give me another chance! It was a joke. I was angry because he had stolen my thunder and that hurt me more than any of his insults before the fight.

I spoke to Eric and he told me to ignore it and get some rest for a few days, which was good advice.

'Michael, why are you bothered about what he says?' he asked me. 'You beat him and millions watched it. Forget it, forget about him, because we have much bigger fish to fry.'

I took a few days out to relax and then I wanted to get straight back in the gym, but first I wanted to enoy my success as the new middleweight champion of the Commonwealth. I bought a metallic red Escort XR3I. The days and weeks after beating Nigel were happy. I had a good time and I had money in the bank. There was no longer any need to watch the pennies, but what I wanted was the money to start working for me. I planned to buy a van and start a removal company and I had the advertising slogan ready: Watson's Removals – We Box Anything. I think that I even had some flyers made and distributed, but in the end I never had enough time to devote to the plan and the idea just faded away.

In the months after beating Nigel my relationship with Zara really fell apart and I could sense that it was going to be increasingly difficult to continue seeing my daughters. I had been a busy and involved dad so it wasn't that – as I see it now, the reason that trouble was brewing was because I had refused to convert to Islam. Zara had become increasingly religious since the birth of our first daughter and I could respect that, but there was simply no way that I could convert. I already had a religion and a belief. I was not, in my opinion, lacking in morals.

The situation between us worsened and became steadily more and more complicated. There were times when I would drive over to see both the girls and sometimes it was hard to leave without them. I would return to my car and just sit there in utter frustration at my total lack of power. In the ring I could tame the most dangerous puncher in Britain, but I was helpless outside the ring as my personal life was falling apart. The relationship had broken down quickly and the crisis with my daughters was an obvious and upsetting side effect.

Though my personal life was suffering, it seemed that my career in the ring was finally moving in the right direction. In July of 1989 I was made the number one contender for McCallum's WBA middleweight title, and Duff told me that he would try and make the match. Duff and his associates had promoted McCallum's victory over Sheffield's Herol Graham for the vacant title, which had taken place just a few days before I had stopped Nigel. McCallum was a slick fighter but surprisingly he had only narrowly beaten Graham, and in my opinion I had the tools to take his title.

The updates from Duff were positive and I was looking forward to winning the world title, having a few more lucrative fights and then hopefully walking away from the business by the time I was twenty-eight. I had my own plans, plans for Mum and plans for my two little girls. I just needed the right fights at the right price and at the right time to totally change the direction of my life. The fight with Benn had raised my profile and I knew that I had to seize the opportunity and cash in on my newfound status.

At about this time a young promoter from Romford called Barry Hearn was starting to make a big impression in the boxing business. He was, like Frank Warren, a rival to Duff and I was, despite growing reservations, a loyal boxer. Duff and I had a contract and to me that was solid as a rock.

At the end of the summer in 1989 I found out that my fight with McCallum was going out to purse bids. This is one of boxing's oldest traditions and it can often lead to boxers receiving big pay-days, so I was quite excited at the news.

A boxer in the number one contender position is entitled to a mandatory challenge against the champion. When a mandatory challenge is due, the sanctioning body, in my case the WBA, announce that the fight will take place and that they will accept purse offers from promoters who are willing to stage the championship contest. Once this procedure has been set in motion the rival promoters of the two boxers, and any others that are interested, will submit their offers in a sealed envelope. The bids will be opened in front of representatives from all involved and the highest bid wins. This can greatly benefit the boxer because he can in theory receive far more for his efforts from a rival promoter than his own promoter or manager has promised him.

If a boxer is not in the mandatory position he is entitled to a voluntary defence. As a rule, the promoter of the champion will almost always promote a voluntary defence. This is because the champion's promoter will want to secure home advantage, and guarantee that the fight remains with a broadcaster that he has a deal with and he will have everything else that comes with being in control of a promotion. I don't want to make scandalous statements, but promoters have been known to influence judges and referees by giving them special treatment. Some have been found guilty of offering bribes, but as far as I know nobody in Britain has ever been charged with bribing an official in a world title fight. Yet!

Duff had promoted McCallum's fight with Graham, and since he promoted me I naturally assumed that he would put the fight on. He told me he would promote it long before I found out about the purse bid, and even after I was aware of the situation he still assured me he would win the bid. It was a shock when I was told that Hearn had won.

When I met Hearn he struck me as a genuine man and I liked him. He told me that he had been a fan of mine for a long time, and that when he saw the fight with McCallum was up for grabs he decided to send in a purse bid. He admitted there was a slightly mischievous element to his involvement.

'To be honest, Michael, I think I caught Mickey by surprise because he thought he had the fight done and dusted, and then they opened my envelope and it was a lot more,' Hearn told me.

It was the second fight in a row that Duff, my manager and my promoter, had lost control of during the bidding and negotiation stages. It disturbed me that Duff had failed to secure the right to promote my two most important fights.

It seemed strange to me that Hearn had even bothered to bid because he did not promote either of us, but he had a few ideas for the future and hopefully I would be involved. He knew I was a star at that time, he knew McCallum was a real world champion and he delivered the fight as a tidy package to ITV. To him it was a business proposition and nothing more, and in that way he was different from Duff, who, for all his faults, saw boxing as more than a business – Duff loved and knew the sport, even if he was difficult to deal with and infuriating at times.

At about this time Hearn had also agreed a promotional deal with a boxer called Chris Eubank, and he introduced his name when talking to me about the future. This was odd because Eubank was unknown and untested, having turned professional in America. Eubank was a good talker and, despite having only had thirteen fights, he was issuing challenges to Benn and me long before our fight. I had heard of him. I had read a profile about him in the first-ever edition of *Boxing Monthly*, which also carried a preview of my fight at Finsbury Park. The profile was a bit over the top, but it was not as bad as the preview and prediction for my fight: Benn was tipped to beat me in one round!

Hearn told me that he was looking to bring Eubank into the equation somewhere down the line in fights against Nigel or me. In the weeks after winning the purse bid, I thought he was mad when he said this. To me, Eubank was a nobody – he was fighting losers, and the fans had already decided that they didn't really like his attitude or style.

We started to prepare for McCallum as soon as we were told that it would take place at Alexandra Palace in North London in November 1989. In all my years of boxing I had never been in better mental or physical shape. I felt so strong that I was easing back in the gym, and as the weeks tumbled by I was growing in confidence. I was blocking out the problems with Zara and focusing all my attention on my training. I watched tapes of McCallum's fight, especially his hard-fought points win over Graham. He was a class act, but I saw gaps and I knew that my condition at that time would be enough to take his title.

When I met Benn I realised just how low-key and old-fashioned I was. I needed to change my image, so before the McCallum fight I had white tracksuits and gowns made for Eric and me with the words *Michael Watson, WBA Middleweight Champion of the World 1989* stitched on them. They were beautiful to look at, and one night I put on a little show for Mum and Uncle Joe at the flat. I felt like a champion just wearing them. Everybody in the flat that night was happy, and with little more than a week or so to go, the sense of anticipation was incredible. I thanked God that I was close to realising a dream and accomplishing a goal. It is difficult to explain – I was not taking McCallum lightly, it was just that I was in absolutely the best condition I had ever been in.

My main sparring partner for the McCallum fight was my old

school friend Ray Webb. I had sparred with Ray at different gyms over the years, but for the McCallum fight I put him on the payroll, as we say in boxing. Ray was paid for sharing the ring with me, and he was good because he was a good mover, tall and lean just like McCallum. As far as I was concerned it was money well spent and he certainly played his part in getting my condition near to perfection.

On the last day of sparring, which was eight days before the fight, I agreed to do six rounds with Ray. I was working on landing punches to Ray's body because McCallum was known as the 'Body Snatcher' and I was planning to give him back some of his own medicine. It was going well, I was moving nicely and getting in under Ray's jabs with ease. He would move off and I would cut the ring down and slip and throw a body punch. Move, slip, punch and get away. It was as easy as walking to me at that stage, second nature.

'Michael, last round and nothing stupid,' Eric called as I came out and touched gloves with Ray.

I was just three minutes away from finishing the hard work when I took off at the start of that last round, and I gently started to circle to Ray's left. The round was nearly over when I moved in and ducked to my right, and as I came back up I felt a terrible pain on my nose. Ray had caught me with a good shot. I immediately backed off and Eric screamed out 'time' before clambering through the ropes. I turned away, and when he grabbed my shoulder and pulled me round to face him, the blood was running down my chin and on to my T-shirt.

Ray came over with a look of fear on his face and Eric was screaming, but nobody was to blame. Perhaps it was my fault for a sloppy move, but the only thing that mattered was that the fight was off. All three of us in the ring knew that it was broken long before the X-ray at the hospital confirmed the damage. I had two black eyes that Sunday when Jamilla and Layla came over, but the real pain was inside because I knew that I had been in the very best condition of my life and now I wouldn't be able to exploit it. I was scared that I would never recapture that state of perfection.

The nose healed and I kept control of my weight over the Christmas period, and by January 1990 I was ready for a new date. I spoke with Duff and he told me that Hearn was talking about a date in April, which was fine, but I wanted a warm-up fight. If I didn't fight until April that would mean that I would have been out of the ring for eleven months, and that is just too long for an active boxer to sit on the sidelines. The ring rust would seriously undermine my chances.

McCallum also knew better than to sit and wait, and in February 1990 he took a voluntary defence against Steve Collins, a tough young fighter from Dublin who was based in Boston. McCallum won on points over twelve rounds – it was a tremendous workout for him.

I was desperate for a warm-up fight so I went to see Hearn and asked him if he could get me on somewhere.

'Mike, don't worry. You'll knock him out because he's an old man. And then you'll do the same to Michael Nunn,' he told me.

At the time Nunn, a gently spoken American, was the International Boxing Federation champion at middleweight and most experts considered him the best of the champions. I knew Hearn was wrong, but there was nothing I could do. I was having a lot of arguments with Duff at the time over a variety of issues. We approached the new date for the McCallum fight with this background.

In the gym my mental strength was perfect but my physical condition was not right. There seemed to be nothing that I could do to get my body back to the shape it had been in before the first fight was postponed. There was something missing, no sparkle in my work, and each night I went over the feelings in my head. I could not quite find an answer to the way I felt, and that is probably because it was the first time that I had struggled to get ready. I knew that I should have insisted on a warm-up and stood my ground, but instead I worked in isolation to get as fit as possible. However, my body was rusty; the timing was off.

The fight was set for 14 April at the Royal Albert Hall, and from the opening bell I felt like I was stuck in a stranger's body. I had never suffered from ring rust before, and it had an immediate and exhausting effect on me. My timing was awful, and that meant I had to go looking for McCallum, and that meant he picked me apart. My night of glory was turning into a painful boxing nightmare. It was a brutal fight and I was forced to stand with him, trading vicious punches, but I was at a massive disadvantage: I had not been in the ring since that night in the tent on Finsbury Park. I was brave, but that is all that can be said. The eleven months out of the ring robbed me of the title as I'd known it would.

I went eleven hard, tough and in the end savage rounds with McCallum that night before he chopped me down. I never tried to run and I never tried to survive. I went in there to win and take his WBA belt, but it was obvious from the beginning that I was fighting a lost cause against a great fighter. In my opinion, and I said this before the fight, McCallum was the best middleweight in the world in 1990 and he had been for a few years. The biggest names from that period, Marvin Hagler, Sugar Ray Leonard, Tommy Hearns and Roberto Duran, all had one thing in common – none of them had ever shared a ring with the 'Body Snatcher'. He caught me on a bad night, but over the years, as our friendship has blossomed, he has admitted to me that he was relieved we never met in 1989 at Alexandra Palace.

I was in a state after the McCallum loss, really bruised and tired. Also, my spirit was on the floor. In the changing room there were various accusations about me going up in weight and doing this wrong and doing that wrong. I just wanted to get out of that place and escape with some friends. I needed some support and comfort.

The following day the girls visited and they were looking at my swollen face and stiff hands. I heard Jamilla ask my mum what was 'wrong with my daddy'. It nearly broke my heart to hear the concern in her voice. When a boxer loses a tough, long fight his body is put through a living hell for twelve rounds and it leaves him swollen and exhausted. It is not pretty, and there is no relief for several days, and when the pain does finally recede, the hurt inside takes over. That was without any doubt the lowest point in my life so far, but I had God to help me through and he did. Mum and Uncle Joe would not let me slip too low.

Then fifteen days after I lost to McCallum I fell a bit lower when I watched ITV in amazement as my old adversary, Nigel Benn, survived a knockdown to win the World Boxing Organisation version of the middleweight title in Atlantic City. Benn ruthlessly stopped Doug DeWitt to reinforce the pain that I was feeling.

I knew that I had a big fight on my hands to get back on top.

I had to try and talk to Duff in an attempt to find some middle ground if our relationship was to continue. Five days after the loss to McCallum I went to his Soho office. He saw me straightaway and immediately started to talk business. He also gave me my cheque for the McCallum fight.

He went over all the old ground and told me what I did wrong and what I had to do now. He talked about two or three fights to get back on the winning track and then another title fight. I was not listening. We parted, and he promised to find me a fight in September and I just nodded. It was a cold meeting but I had expected that.

I waited until I had left his office before I opened the envelope. I was shocked because the amount was less than I had got for my previous fight. My anger was growing. I wanted to go back and demand the rest of my money, but I just went home.

Duff had been in charge of my career for nearly six years, but that day on a street corner in Soho when I looked at the cheque, I knew it was over.

When I had first been to his office with Mum and Uncle Joe we had sat and listened to his plans for me and believed him. We had placed our faith and my career in his hands and let him get on with it. If I had a difficult fight, I accepted his reasoning, and if he blamed me I took the blame. He was my manager and my promoter and we had a contract from one of British sport's oldest governing bodies. He made the fights and I won them, he organised the money and he gave me my share. I had my share in my hand from the beating that McCallum had given me and it was not enough. I wanted more and I knew how to get it: I had to take control of my own career.

Before I could break away I would have to make legal history and somehow get out of the British Boxing Board of Control's standard boxer-manager-promoter contract. I mentioned to a few people in the business that I was planning on breaking the contract and leaving Duff, but nobody believed that I could walk away. It had never happened before and Duff was a powerful man, a man who knew what he could and couldn't do. In the boxing business a fighter was connected to his manager via the contract and that was that back then. Nobody considered it illegal, and nobody had been able to change it. I wanted to change it, but I was not leading a campaign to alter the rules and regulations of boxing, I wanted to change it for Michael Watson. I wanted to be free to negotiate my own fights and my own deals, and that was all I was concerned about. It was selfish, but then boxing is a selfish sport.

I went to see Ambrose Mendy because I wanted to seek his advice. Nigel was in America preparing for a world title defence in Las Vegas against former champion Iran Barkley. Both Mendy and Benn were back under the spotlight and they were big, big news. I had to wait in his lobby to see him and with every second that ticked by I kept on thinking back to the night in the tent on Finsbury Park. It was just a year earlier, but leaving the ring that night with the Commonwealth belt seemed like ancient history to me. It made me crazy to think that Nigel had walked away that night with his pride and reputation in tatters and yet, at this very moment, he was in Las Vegas entertaining the world's press. Nigel knocked out Barkley in one round in a sensational fight that raised his profile even higher. What a crazy reversal in fortunes. It was a good thing I still had my faith and my belief, because there were times when I had to turn to prayer to keep sane.

Ambrose treated me with respect and he had all the right connections. We had a good chat and he did suggest a guy called Ross Hemsworth. I knew absolutely nothing about Hemsworth and I was not in a hurry to call him and find out.

In August 1990 Duff offered me a fight at York Hall in September on one of his own shows. Although I had just been beaten, there was no way I was getting back in the ring against an American journeyman for the money on offer. I had made £100,000 for the Benn fight – that is, before any deductions. The final figure I received for the McCallum fight was still a controversial subject and one that was really annoying me. I went back to Duff and told him that the money was not enough for the fight at York Hall. We disagreed about it. I listened, but my mind was elsewhere. I'm sure that was the last telephone conversation we ever had. I rejected the fight because I deserved more money, and I wanted the right to go and negotiate for more money. I had the courage of my convictions and so I decided to take matters into my own hands.

On 7 September 1990 I initiated proceedings against Duff, who I had to sue under his real name of Morris Prager, for restraint of trade with regard to our contract. I wanted to get out and make my own decisions. I knew I faced a court battle that would be every bit as brutal and draining as a major title fight. Henri Brandman, my new solicitor, who had previously been Benn's solicitor during the negotiations for our fight, warned me that it would not be easy, that a victory would be extremely hard to achieve.

Some of the press had started to call me and Eric because they had heard rumours that I had split with Duff. We both denied the tales but it was clear that I needed a press conference to clear the air and put across my point of view. I found the number that Ambrose had given me for Ross Hemsworth and gave him a call. A conference was arranged for 18 September at a hotel in London's West End. I was determined to be as relaxed as possible. There was a large turnout of press and I guessed that it would not be easy, but Hemsworth, who seemed confident, dealt with a lot of the aggressive questions very well.

'Michael has nothing to do with either Barry Hearn or Ambrose Mendy,' Hemsworth told the press pack.

'Michael manages his own career from this point forward and I can confirm that a writ has been issued against Mickey Duff,' he continued.

The press boys were lapping it up because they love a good scrap between rival promoters, especially an extra juicy one where the prize is a leading boxer. They also sensed that legal proceedings would be different from normal because the case would be played out in a public court and not behind closed doors at the British Boxing Board of Control's offices. They knew me, so they knew this was not an idle threat. I had dumped Duff and they all knew how serious that was.

'I will advise Michael about his financial position and be available when and if he needs any other advice,' Hemsworth insisted. He added that he had been accused of many things and would be seeking legal advice in response to such claims.

The boxing writers seemed content with Hemsworth's claims, but then they turned their attention to my future. They wanted to know what, as a self-managed fighter, I was going to do. I have to admit I had not really devised a plan because it was all happening a bit too quick for me, and I hadn't had time to take a step back and think about the future. I knew the type of fights I wanted, but to tell the truth I was not even sure who my future promoter would be.

'I have seen a list of fighters,' I offered. It was clearly a stalling tactic.

Before the conference Hemsworth had briefly told me about one particular plan of his, and I had listened as he explained the possible route that I could take. The reporters were heating up – they wanted names and dates and schedules because back then a boxing press conference was only called to give out information. I understand it is very different now, but on that afternoon the pack wanted some facts and figures. Hemsworth took over and started to outline the next twelve months of my boxing career, beginning with a fight in October 1990 and ending with a fight in the summer of 1991. He announced that I would clear £2.5 million in total. There is nothing the boxing press likes more than a nice thick figure, and in 1990 £2.5 million was a lot of cash!

'A major American boxing promoter has made the offer to us and we have put together a realistic schedule for Michael to become the number one middleweight in the world by the end of the summer of 1991,' Hemsworth continued.

Eric was with me on the top table and the pair of us just kept on smiling because we were not really sure where the conversation and the claims were going. I was asked about the American promoter and I replied that I couldn't say too much. However, Hemsworth, who was really starting to enjoy himself, said that it was Bob Arum, who at that time was promoting Nigel Benn's American fights. Arum and Don King were the giants of boxing then, a pair of untouchable men with the power to move mountains, slice open oceans and make impossible fights happen.

Hemsworth told the reporters that the October fight would

just be a warm-up and that in December I would meet the Boston-based Dubliner Steve Collins, who had earlier that year survived twelve hard rounds with McCallum. There was, according to Hemsworth, another easy fight planned for early January in America, and then in the spring of 1991 I would have a rematch with Benn. The final fight of the five would be a middleweight unification showdown at Wembley Stadium against Michael Nunn in the summer. It was a grand scheme, but I knew enough about the way the business of boxing worked to know that it was more hype than truth.

Colin Hart, boxing correspondent with the *Sun*, asked Eric what he thought about the planned fights.

'Eric, if you don't mind me saying so, this all sounds too good to be true and I was wondering, are you going to stay with Michael?' enquired Harty. His phrasing may have been slightly more colourful.

'I will go with my boxer – I came into boxing with Michael and I will go out of boxing with him,' Eric replied.

Another dozen or so questions were asked about the dates and finances for the five fights, and Hemsworth did his best to keep the dream going. I know that we had not quite made firm believers of the writers, but we had given them a lot of stories.

I was asked about the fight at York Hall that Duff had arranged for me. The rumour was that I had accepted and then wriggled out of. It was the start of the misinformation that would dominate my life for the next six months or so.

A few days after the press conference I was firmly back on my own, and then, in October 1990, I made contact with Barry Hearn.

At the time Hearn was busy putting the last touches to a fight between Nigel Benn and Chris Eubank at the NEC in Birmingham on 18 November. I finally managed to get a meeting with him at his Romford office and we agreed a deal that included me being hastily placed on the Benn-Eubank undercard. It seemed like a bad joke. I was the eliminator for two boxers I had already beaten, but what else could I do? I either had to stay with Duff, or I had to go along with nice guy Hemsworth and his multimillion-pound dream. I signed a promotional deal with Hearn because it made sense.

The letters were flying between Brandman and Duff's solicitors but I had to forget about all of that and get my head and body right for the eighteenth and a fight against a dangerous opponent. There was no messing about with Hearn, and he came up with Errol Christie for my return to the ring. Christie was once the golden boy of the sport but he had lost some crucial fights, and his best days were behind him. However, he was still hungry and that made him a risk. But I was optimistic and felt that I was in good shape. I just had to beat him and await the outcome of the Benn-Eubank fight. I had less than three weeks to get ready.

The fight against Christie at the NEC, Birmingham was easy. Hearn had warned me that he was not going to get me a string of meaningless wins, and he was right. On paper the win over

Christie was good and it raised my profile again inside the trade. Now that I had beaten Christie I hoped I would get my chance at Eubank.

I had been known as the People's Choice at the time of the fight with Nigel but I was now being called the People's Champion.

After the Christie fight I agreed a long-term deal with Hearn. The deal included a chance to fight Eubank, providing both boxers could agree terms. There was no guarantee of a fight with the new champion, and I would have to wait for him to select me as one of his challengers, but the chance existed and that was enough for me. I had moved a step higher in my mind, a step in the right direction, but I now had to deal with Duff and our court case.

I was told that I would be in court in February 1991, and then I was told that I would finally get to defend my Commonwealth title on 23 January. I was ready for both confrontations, and once again Christmas went out the window. I did buy the girls presents, but it was difficult to see them and when I eventually did get to spend some time with them there was precious little of it.

The opponent for my January fight was an Australian called Craig Trotter who looked like George Michael. We fought at the Brentwood Leisure Centre. He was brave and took some heavy shots before he retired after five rounds with a suspected broken jaw. Even before I left the arena I was being reminded by my lawyer, Henri Brandman, to look at the notes for the case. Hearn agreed not to make a fight for me until I was free from Duff and out of the British Boxing Board of Control's contract.

I spent a lot of time preparing for the court case and I knew I had to be mentally strong. I prayed hard and put my faith in God. Mum and Uncle Joe also gave me a lot of support and prayed with me. It was going to be a testing time, but I knew I would pull through.

We had to prove that the British Boxing Board of Control's contract was unenforceable on the basis that it was in restraint of trade. We also had to prove that a promoter who also acts as a manager negotiates with himself, and that that was wrong. We spent hours going over all the details and all the angles we thought Duff's legal team would use. We were ready when the time came for me to face Duff at the Royal Courts of Justice in the Strand.

We were in court on February 19, 20, 21, 22 and 25 and I was there every day. It was tiring and there were times when it seemed to be going against us, but we stood our ground defiantly. It was never scary facing Duff in court because I always believed justice would be done and that gave me the strength I needed whenever I was called to the witness box. Once again Mum and Uncle Joe were at my side.

The judge, Mr Justice Scott, listened each day without betraying his feelings. It was hard to gauge what he was thinking. At the end of each session and at the end of each day, Brandman would shake his head as often as he smiled and I really had no indication of whether or not he thought we were winning.

After five very long days it was finished and a date was set for the judgement a couple of weeks later. The wait was terrible. There was no clear sign that my fight would be over when we returned to the Courts on 15 March.

I was more nervous on the morning of the judgement than I had ever been in a fight. Nobody spoke a word as we drove from the flat to Strand.

We won. The case went against Duff because the judge decided that the BBBofC's contract should have provided the boxer with the right to negotiate. I had set a legal precedent and the case exists in the Law Reports for the year as a leading authority on whether an agreement is unenforceable as declared in restraint of trade. But most of all I just felt great relief that it was over and that I was free. Now I could get on with my life and my career.

The decision was a piece of history and I was very aware of what this meant not just for me, but for all boxers. The Board changed their contract after the case and added a new clause that gave boxers the right to negotiate.

After the victory against Duff I was back in the gym and looking forward to whatever Hearn could arrange for me. I wanted a title and Eubank had one. If I could secure a fight and beat him, I knew I would be the biggest star in British boxing. It was twenty-two months since my win over Benn, and now that I'd finished with Duff I could not see any obstacles standing between me fulfilling my dream of winning a world title.

I had a quick fight at York Hall on 1 May when I knocked out Anthony Brown in less than two minutes of Round One. It was not much of a fight, just a simple way to get rid of any cobwebs and the ring rust that had ruined my chance in the McCallum fight.

Before the Brown fight I had travelled with Brandman to Romford to see Hearn and talk about the only fight that mattered to me. I had left that meeting with a date for a world title fight against Eubank. I was set, I was happy, I was free. I felt optimistic and very determined. I was totally focused. There was only one thought on my mind – to take Eubank's belt.

Chapter 6

I agreed terms to meet Eubank at Earl's Court 2 in a challenge for his World Boxing Organisation middleweight title on 21 June 1991. There was instant interest and the fight was given the title 'By Public Demand' by Barry Hearn's pressman, Andy Ayling. From the very first day news started to leak out, I was once again thrust head first into the type of media scrutiny I had not experienced since before the Nigel Benn fight two years earlier.

A press conference to officially announce the contest was held at the Grosvenor House Hotel in May. Again, there was a media frenzy. Eubank and I had come face-to-face before the conference, but there had been no exchange of words. We would do our verbal sparring in front of the cameras. There was never a dull moment when we sat down to meet the press.

Hearn anticipated a sell-out crowd of 11,000 and that suited me perfectly. I had about six or seven weeks to get right, and I had a hard decision to make. I had been with Eric for about eight years but I needed something extra for the Eubank fight. I was determined not to make the mistakes I had made against McCallum. In many ways the fight with Eubank was far more important – if I lost to Eubank it was difficult to see where I could go in the future, so I decided that getting a bit of extra help with my training was crucial. I told Eric I wanted to bring somebody else in. Of course he was not pleased about this and probably felt hurt, but I felt I needed a different strategy, which I didn't think Eric could provide.

I knew the man I wanted to bring. My mind was made up and since I had gone to court to get control of my career, it was up to me to do just that.

I picked up the phone and called Jimmy Tibbs at his home and we arranged to meet the following day in a café that I had often been to for a meal after sparring a few years earlier, when I first turned professional and would go over to a gym above the Royal Oak pub in Canning Town. At that time Jimmy was training Mark Kaylor – I put in a lot of rounds with Kaylor, who was a tough and powerful fighter. Jimmy and I had got on well and I always found time to stop and chat with him whenever we bumped into each other on the circuit.

I asked Jimmy if he would come in and help me prepare for the fight, and he accepted. I knew that he was a good trainer and a good motivator. He told me not to get overconfident or too relaxed and, most importantly, not to underestimate Eubank. It was very good advice.

'Eubank's fearless and that makes him dangerous,' Jimmy warned me.

I set up a gym in Tottenham, close to White Hart Lane, and worked on breaking up Eubank's rhythm and getting on top of him without leaving myself exposed on the way in. The preparation was excellent and the weight was coming down nicely, but the weight remained an issue because after the McCallum defeat Duff had told the press I was too big for the middleweight limit of eleven stone six pounds, and that I was moving up to the new weight of super-middleweight, which is an increase of eight pounds.

There was a final press conference at the Café Royal in Regent Street ten days before the fight. In the fight poster I was billed as 'The Force', a nickname given to me because of the power of my punches. I also had another name at the time of the first fight with Eubank: I was being called the People's Champion.

I had picked up a lot of new fans when it became known that I was a fan of Arsenal football club, where Eric worked as steward. I could walk from Mum's flat to Highbury in about fifteen minutes, and had played charity football matches at Highbury. Kevin Campbell was one of my friends, as was the sadly missed David 'Rocky' Rocastle.

The weigh-in for the Eubank fight was scheduled for the Odeon, Leicester Square at 9.30 in the morning. It was a major event and thankfully we arrived early, because when I took a check-weight I was about one pound above the eleven stone six pound limit. Eric and Jimmy looked stunned, but I was calm. I knew what I had eaten, and what liquids I had taken in, so I knew I could drop a pound easily. I had taken the precaution of packing a skipping rope and some training kit. We found a warm and quiet basement room below the cinema's screen and I eased into a quick session with one eye on the clock, because in boxing a fighter has to make the agreed weight at the agreed time or forfeit his right to the title or the challenge. I was not going to get in the ring that night with Eubank just for bragging rights. I wanted his World Boxing Organisation middleweight title and the belt that came with the territory. I had an hour to make the weight. I started skipping.

By the time I stepped on the scales, hundreds of people had filled the Odeon and there were chants of 'Wat-son, Wat-son.' I made the weight.

At Earl's Court that night I had my own Portakabin for use as a changing area, which suited me because it helped my concentration. Kamel, a friend who had been helping out, was there, plus one or two other close friends, and of course Jimmy and Eric were in position. There was a feeling of intensity that night, a level of expectation that set me just a bit more on edge than normal. All the talking and interviews were over – this was the real thing, and outside the thin walls of my temporary changing room I could hear the fans shouting.

The WBO's officials checked and rechecked my bandages and my gloves, and then I heard the familiar call from Ernie Draper, the whip for the night: 'Michael, ten minutes.' Draper had been knocking on my dressing-room doors and putting his head round them since I had turned pro. I was ready long before the door opened and the security for the night stepped in and asked me to leave with them. The ITV cameras were on me from the moment I stepped outside the hut and they followed me to the ring through the biggest and noisiest crowd I had ever seen. I was stunned by the reception.

In the ring I kept moving and kept my body working because I didn't want to lose the sweat I had worked up in the changing area. After a few minutes Eubank's theme song, 'Simply The Best', filled the arena and then he appeared. He looked calm as he made his way, very slowly, to the ring, and once he had completed his familiar vault over the top rope I went and got in his face. I admit that the event was getting my blood flowing, and the referee, an American called Frank Cappuccino, ordered me back to my corner.

At the start of the first round I was a bit too eager to get at Eubank, and I missed with a lot of punches. I knew I had to calm down, and I did as the rounds went by. At the halfway stage I was in front in my mind, but not by much. I was making Eubank fight for longer periods in the rounds than other fighters had been able to, and that would, I thought, leave him tired in the later rounds.

A lot has been written about the last half of my first fight with Eubank, and nobody doubts that I won that part of the fight clearly. At the end of the ninth round I told Eric I was enjoying myself, but he sensibly warned against relaxing too much.

His words made me focus, and in Round Ten I had Eubank hurt, and he was forced back to the ropes and made to cover up. Eubank has told me since that I should have finished him in that round because he was in trouble, and I told him that I did try to finish him! In the final round I summoned up a last effort after Jimmy had told me to keep moving, keep jabbing.

'Stick to it, Michael, and you're the new world champion,' he told me.

At the final bell I turned to my corner and walked into the arms of Jimmy and Eric. We had done it. All the preparation had paid off, and far from quitting, as Eubank had said I would, I had taken the fight to him and won his belt clearly. In my mind I was the world champion, and as I walked around the ring, nodding at the press guys and photographers I knew, I had absolutely no sense of the drama that would unfold. I had given him a lesson, made him face reality.

Eubank came over to me during the break between the final bell and the announcement. His face was bruised and he looked exhausted.

'You're a great fighter,' he told me.

I thanked him, and then we each went to our corners to wait for the verdict. Jimmy wiped away the remnants of a slight nose-bleed and took another look at the grazing under my left eye. I had gone twelve hard rounds for the first time in my life, and I felt exhilarated. If I had prepared the same way and been in the same mental and physical condition for the McCallum fight, I would never have ended up flat on my back in Round Eleven.

There was a long delay before the ring announcer took the microphone to read out the verdict. I thought I saw one of Eubank's minders smiling, and that set my mind racing. Surely the judges couldn't deny me the title? Eubank had never stopped trying, it was true, but I was simply too skilful for him and knew too many ways to overcome his strengths.

'We have a split decision . . .'

That was all I heard, and it was all I needed to hear because I knew then, in my own mind, that I had been robbed.

He was still the champion, and I was the loser once again in a world title fight, but this time the decision was wrong and before long I realised that I was not the only one who thought it was unfair.

'What do I have to do to win? was all I could say repeatedly, in disbelief.

Eric was convinced that I had won every round, and Jimmy told me that I had done more than enough to deserve the win. Chris knew that I was the better boxer in that fight and has said since that all he wanted to do was survive and walk out of the ring on his feet.

I felt completely cheated. I had used all my reserves and strength and skill against Chris. I had done everything right – and still it had ended in a wrong decision.

I was very low in spirit. The decision seemed incomprehensible. I was wrecked, physically and mentally. I went to a friend's flat where I knew few people would be able to reach me. I needed time alone so I could find peace of mind again.

The phone calls started early the next day, even though nobody was meant to know where I was staying. Mum had given Mike McCallum my number, and he called to let me know that he thought I had won. I appreciated his kind words, but the fact remained that I had lost, and even a brief look at the papers failed to lift my spirits. The Sundays carried fight reports but, because of the time constraints of deadlines, lacked analysis of the outrage.

I spoke with Mum and she told me that neighbours, friends and the press had been knocking on the door and telephoning all night long. I could believe her, and with the realisation that a lot of people felt upset for me, I set about putting it right. I was going to demand a rematch.

The newspapers on Monday morning, 24 June, were packed with outraged reports on the fight and the injustice that I had suffered. It lifted me because in my wildest dreams I could not have imagined that there would be such public support for me. The *Sun* and the *Daily Mirror* ran several pages of stories and features, and the message was the same: Watson was robbed.

I had decided to organise a conference off my own back and without the support of my promoter, Barry Hearn. I was self-managed and I had earned the right to make decisions for myself. I had no idea what type of reception or turnout there would be, and kept an open mind as I approached the kerb outside.

A reporter I was friends with greeted me and we walked through the gathered press pack and found an empty office to have a quick talk. He told me that the British Boxing Board of Control wanted to support my call for a rematch and planned to lobby the WBO on my behalf. The feeling of desolation I had felt since the decision was announced was finally starting to be replaced by optimism. If there was a rule somewhere that granted me a rematch, I knew I would get the chance, and the press told me that they would all get behind it. Even the few reporters who thought I'd lost wanted to see the pair of us fight again.

The *Daily Mirror* had asked readers to phone in their opinion on whether Eubank deserved to win. Eubank managed just 1,294 votes but 9,658 votes, nearly 90 per cent of all the people that picked up the phone, decided that I was the uncrowned middleweight champion. The rest of the papers followed a similar path and called for a rematch. The pressure was mounting on the WBO and Hearn to get together and agree a deal.

Eubank had kept quiet during the fallout but I heard that he was growing increasingly angry at the support I was receiving. In the days after the fight he started to claim that he had won clearly. He dismissed me by saying that my best asset was 'durability', but I was getting far too much favourable coverage to be bothered by his words.

I met with Hearn and Brandman and the deal was agreed. A press conference was called for 17 July at White Hart Lane football ground, the home of Arsenal's arch rivals Tottenham Hotspur – the fight would take place there on 21 September.

It was to become a monumental date in my life. A day I thought I would never forget, but also a day that I can't remember.

Chapter 7

Before the first fight with Eubank there had been a high level of media interest, but the fuss that was being made about the rematch was something else. Within days of leaving Barry Hearn's office the secret was out and the phones were ringing nonstop with requests for interviews and sessions with photographers. I had to walk away from the glitz for a few days because I had some personal business to sort out and I knew it would not be pleasant.

The decision to bring in Jimmy Tibbs to help in the corner before the first fight had, I thought, been the right one. Jimmy was a cool head, a seasoned pro, and I truly believed that his involvement had helped me that night against Eubank. But I was faced with a dilemma between loyalty to Eric, who had been with me since I'd first switched to Colvestone, and the obvious, professional and sensible choice of upgrading Jimmy to my main trainer. I hadn't fallen out with Eric at the time, but I knew I needed more than he could give me.

Eric was upset with the new arrangement and that was the end of our time together.

Over the years I have lost contact with Eric and I am sad about the way our relationship ended.

Once I had sorted out the situation with Eric I met with Jimmy and agreed a fee with him for the fight. Jimmy would use Dean Powell, a young trainer he had been working with for a few years, as his assistant, who would have to be paid. Now that I was in charge of my career I had to be sensible with the money. Jimmy was on money, Jon Robinson was on a fee for working as my agent on the fight, and I would also have to pay all additional training costs in the period leading to the fight. The buck, as they say, stopped with me. I had to pay my own way and I was getting a fast lesson in the economics of the boxing business.

Jimmy decided that we would train at the West Ham Amateur Boxing gym in Plaistow, which is behind the Black Lion pub near the tube station. It was a proper gym and I knew there would be a lot of fighters in and out of the place who would provide me with different styles of sparring. I knew the place, I'd sparred there a few times over the years and it was perfect for us.

The rematch was not going to be for Eubank's WBO middleweight title but for the WBO's vacant super-middleweight title. It was an increase of eight pounds, from eleven stone six pounds to twelve stone, and it suited both boxers, even if we insisted that we could continue to make the middleweight limit. Eubank spoke boldly of going back down to middleweight and regaining his old belt so that he would have two titles after winning the rematch against me.

During the first week of July the September fight seemed like a long way off, but I had a lot of unfinished business to tidy up before I became a training recluse. I had bought a semi-detached house in Chingford in January 1991 and I needed to do a few things there because I was staying there full time and I needed it to feel more like a home. I roped in a couple of mates to help with the decorating. I wanted it to be a nice place for my children when they came. It had a back garden, so they would be able to play outside. I felt proud that I could give my daughters a bit more than I had had in my childhood.

The upcoming fight was generating publicity long before the posters went up all over London. On the day of the conference I travelled over to White Hart Lane with Jimmy and we took our seats at the table. The trophy room at the ground was packed with reporters and film crews and once again, just like at the Grosvenor a few months earlier, we went outside to have pictures taken first. Eubank, as usual, looked away and pretended to be bored. It was an act and I laughed like I always did whenever he tried to annoy me. I knew that laughter was a weapon that Eubank had no defence against because he took his act so seriously.

It was 17 July and it was without doubt the most explosive conference we had so far taken part in.

I took my time and told him that the first fight had scared him so much that he had done everything in his power to avoid a rematch.

We finished up the hard gym work a few days after the conference and I thanked Gary Delaney and Chris Pyatt, both of whom had helped me, for their efforts in the sparring. I was ready, and Jimmy and Dean seemed happy. I was looking forward to doing the job professionally and getting Eubank out of my system once and for all. I was even looking forward to the night after the fight, when I planned on attending a dinner at the Grosvenor House Hotel in honour of special guest Muhammad Ali. Jon, my agent, had a table and Jimmy and I were due to go with him. It was going to be quite a weekend.

The plan for the fight weekend was neatly organised. On the Friday I would travel with Kamel from my house in Chingford to the Hyde Park Hotel in Knightsbridge for a nice, restful sleep. The hotel was particularly plush and our suite was spacious, which was just as well because quite a few friends came by, including Jim and Dawn, my special dietitians. Jimmy and Dean had a suite on the same floor, and it all added up to a different level of professionalism. After I had eaten some food that Mum had prepared for me, I went out for a quiet but companionable stroll with Kamel.

Back at the hotel I went in to see Jimmy and Dean. I prayed with Jimmy, because he was a born-again Christian like me, and then I went back to my room to sleep. Eubank had been on my mind for months, but on the night before the rematch I was calm. I spoke to Mum before going to bed, and that night I had no dreams. I just went off to sleep peacefully, knowing that my faith in Jesus would get me through any difficulties I would encounter.

The next morning when I arrived at the house in Chingford a crowd was gathering, and Mum and Uncle Joe served up a treat for us. There was my DJ friend, Tim Westwood, Kamel, Jimmy, Dean and a few other close, close friends. We ate like kings in my front room and the atmosphere was fantastic. Dean went to get the papers and we had a brief look through them – it seemed like they were split about fifty-fifty. I was not bothered by the split because I was the 'people's champion', like it said on the poster, and I had the people on my side.

I went up the stairs on my own at about 1 p.m. for a rest. It was the last time I would walk to my bedroom without assistance for nearly a decade.

There were less than ten hours to go before my life changed for ever.

The limo came before six that evening and I was ready, in the living room, talking and joking with Tim. Jimmy and Dean were hovering over the table checking and rechecking their kit and my bag, putting in the essential items and filling any extra spaces with towels. There was a gumshield, protective cup, spare gumshield, and boots. The shorts and gown were on a separate hanger, neat, new and crisp.

Jimmy and Dean had their own special tools and gadgets for stopping any cuts that I might suffer, and these were placed carefully in what looked like a washbag. The smell of Mum's spaghetti bolognese was still hovering in the air.

Mum had gone home to get ready with some of her friends from the Evering church, and Uncle Joe had remained with me.

He led a quick prayer in my living room before we went out and climbed in the limo, Tim, Uncle Joe, Dean, Kamel, Jimmy and me.

The car had tinted windows, and as we approached the venue we could all see the fans walking towards the turnstiles. It felt like a big occasion, and as we got closer and the car went slower, people started to guess who was inside. When we stopped outside the main gates, the crowd was chanting my name. Eubank had a police escort from the Grosvenor.

I got out and waved through the gates at the fans. They were chanting my name: 'Wat-son, Wat-son, Wat-son.' It was ringing in my ears, thumping deep inside my head, and I heard it all night long.

I had agreed at the last press conference to use the visitors' changing room because as an Arsenal fan I had no desire to change in the home dressing room. It was just a short walk from the main gates to the changing rooms, and once inside we took up our positions. It felt familiar because we had taken a look at it already, and Jimmy had it all worked out – he knew where he was going to do my hands and what wall he was going to use for gently placing all of the different pieces of tape that are needed to hold the bandage firm and protect the fists of a fighter. A trainer covers the wall with dozens of pieces of tape, and when he is putting the bandages on he just reaches up and plucks a small strip from the wall and places it across a part of the band-age, and then continues winding the bandage around the fist. It is a long process, but it is very calming and it allows the trainer and the fighter some time alone. Dean moved a few chairs to create a bit more space so that I could shadow-box when I had to.

After a short time, Jimmy put a stop to all the people who were coming in and out of the changing room. Jimmy spoke with me, reminding me quietly about what we had spent two months perfecting. We talked about working for three minutes, going back with my hands held high and keeping an eye open for Eubank's counters. We also spoke about keeping faith, and then we started to prepare because it was getting closer and closer to the 9.50 start time.

I was so calm that I could see I was making Jimmy a bit nervous about my relaxed mood. To me it was my big night, it was that simple, and there was no way that Eubank could hurt me or beat me.

I have watched the next fifty minutes of my life dozens of times since it happened.

First, for five minutes there is my ring walk and then Eubank's ring walk, followed by the introductions. Most of the cheers are for me, but Eubank had a lot of fans there too, which seemed to surprise people.

Then there are thirty-three minutes and twenty-nine seconds of boxing, and a total of ten single minutes of me sitting on my stool in the corner between rounds and looking up into Jimmy's eyes.

When the fight is called off there are several more minutes of confusion, and then nothing – just months and years that are gone for ever.

When I watch the tape, there are parts that I can remember, quick flashes of recognition, each time I sit down. I started having those moments from the very first day that I ever watched it, and that was long before I could talk or walk or remember anything else. My mind is always sharper after I watch the rematch.

This is what I have watched over the years, and how I view it.

Round One: Eubank tries to land a few lazy jabs, but I move in with my own rights and many of them connect. I can push him back, he's not as strong as he was in the first fight. Or I'm just so much stronger. The crowd is chanting my name and Eubank is talking to me. (I know now what he was saying but I would never repeat it.) The fighting is done. I finish with a short left and a right, which he blocks. At the bell I get close to his face and growl. The crowd love it, I love it. Round One to me.

Round Two: I go straight back at him, but I'm too eager and he catches me with a left hook that forces me back a pace. I call him in and smile, and then dominate the rest of the round. I'm putting him under pressure, and even if he is blocking some of the punches, enough are getting through. I remember what Mike McCallum said to me a few days earlier. He told me to sit on Eubank the whole time and never give him a rest. I do and even when I'm in a clinch with him I never settle long enough for him to land a punch. Round Two to me.

Round Three: My biggest round so far. Eubank looks like he's tired, tired of running and trying to get away from my punches. I'm mixing my attacks from body to head and I chase him all over the ring. I catch him with a cracking right near the end of the round and at the bell I look over at him. It's going to plan – my plan and Jimmy's plan. Eubank has been put under constant pressure for nine minutes and it's painfully obvious that he's struggling. Round Three to me.

Round Four: Early in the round I cut Eubank's left eyebrow with a short right and I can immediately see the blood. Eubank never flinches when the blood starts to trickle down his cheek. The crowd start to chant my name again, but Eubank has been severely shouted at by Ronnie Davies in the corner and he starts to counter my rushes. There is suddenly a degree of urgency in his punches, and he catches me with one good left hook. I shrug the punch off, but it is his best round so far. Round Four to Eubank.

Round Five: Jimmy has told me to close the gap and not to stand and look at my work. I get closer before throwing my combinations, and when I let go there are five or six in each flurry. Eubank has no reply, and by the end of the round he looks weary and confused. Nigel Benn is ringside, screaming for me. (When he was interviewed he predicted that Eubank would not last the pace.) Eubank looks exhausted, but he still wastes fifteen seconds strutting at the end of each round instead of going back and sitting down for a breather. Round Five to me.

Round Six: We both slip over in this round – I lose my balance, and Eubank looks like he goes over because he's breathing heavily. I work my way forward with jabs and then slicing rights that force Eubank to scurry away. I put together my best combination of the fight when I connect with a left uppercut and a right cross and sweat and blood fly from Eubank's face after impact. Commentators Barry McGuigan and Jimmy McDonnell predict that Eubank will be stopped. (Eubank told his trainer, Ronnie, that I was too strong for him when he did finally sit down during the break.) Round Six to me.

Round Seven: Each round is starting slower than the previous one, but I'm not tired, not tiring. I am looking for ways to break this proud man down. I know he will never quit, and as my rights over his jab and short hooks under his guard connect, I also know that he is capable of firing back the occasional punch. His chin and his heart are quite amazing. His loose left hooks are a problem because they come from hidden angles and land behind my guard. He can tell that his punches are not hurting me, and that makes him despondent. His head is starting to go down, I am slowly getting to his spirit. I don't think that I miss him with a right counter in the

round. I pick up a small nick by my left eye. Round
Seven to me.

Round Eight: In the corner Jimmy is still talking about
patience – he wants me to keep the pressure on but not go
too crazy. Eubank comes at me, and for the first minute
we are locked in the middle of the ring. He is defiantly
standing his ground and taking a lot of punches, but he is
also connecting with his own. (He claimed that at the end
of the previous round he had stopped feeling sorry for
himself.) I meet his resistance and he soon starts to back
away. The crowd stand and chant my name. I keep my
head and follow him with short rights and quick lefts. I
know that he has no reply from his back foot, but
knowing that and being able to take advantage of the
weakness are two very different things. I have him backed
up, and from that position his rights over the top have no
effect on me. Round Eight to me.

Round Nine: (Eubank once claimed that by Round Nine I
was keeping him up and making him suffer, but that is
nonsense. He claimed I was humiliating him on purpose,
which is not true. I would never do a thing like that. I
wanted him out of there and I looked for openings at all
times to end the fight.) He has little strength in this round
and is sent reeling again and again from my punches. (I
suppose I was enjoying beating him, but I would prefer to
have stopped him and put an end to the night.) I am

doing what I want, but I just can't land the knockout punch or enough clean shots to drop him. Round Nine to me.

Round Ten: The referee, Roy Francis, has to put his hand on my chest to stop me going out too early. I watch images of me bouncing and moving with speed and ease all over the ring. Eubank seems helpless when I counter his lunges, and again and again he avoids me by ducking low. The crowd starts chanting, and when Eubank misses with a big right near the bell I pounce and send him back to his corner with a couple of shots bouncing around in his head. He has nothing left, my guard is down, and even my corner tones down its words of caution when I sit down. Nobody knows what is keeping Eubank in the fight. He is getting hit five or six shots to one, and his punches have not bothered in any round. Round Ten to me.

Round Eleven: The greatest round. Eubank catches me early and I end up on the ropes, but it is not the right and the left that send me back. It is not the clubbing, desperate punches that force me to lean back across the ropes. My head looks clear to me at that point. The hurt is caused by the best right he has ever thrown, when for once he measures my attack, steps forward and lets it go. He hits me with a hard, short right that twists my head and sends me reeling to the ropes. I am stunned, but not out on my feet. That punch was lethal, and in slow motion it just gets better and better.

I come off the ropes and recover, and then he is tired and I take over. The fight looks over and Eubank suddenly appears close to voluntary collapse. I force him back and land a left over his guard. I move in with another left and then a cracking right on the side of his head and cheek. I see him slip to his right knee after the right connects, but it is the punch that drops him. The mighty Eubank is down and there is pandemonium at ringside and all over the ground. It is said that twenty-two thousand people were there and twelve million were watching on ITV. They all saw Eubank fall to his knee near the end of Round Eleven.

The referee moves forward after sending me to a neutral corner. Eubank regains his feet quickly and then the ref motions for us to 'box on'. Time stops; it does whenever I watch the tape. He gets up. His body looks finished and his eyes glazed. I come out of the neutral corner after a glance at Jimmy in my corner. I know I am thinking the title is mine, I know I am thinking the dream has nearly come true, and I know that I am thinking that my two lovely girls, Jamilla and Layla, will never have to worry again. Daddy has won the world title for them. I know I was thinking all of these things because what else would I have been thinking about?

I see the referee's hands motion for us to start fighting again. I move forward. One second. I pull my hands up.

Two seconds. I set myself to throw a right. Three
seconds. I can see his right fist. Four seconds. It rips
through my guard and connects cleanly under my chin.
I'm going back, falling. Five seconds. I hit the second
rope with the back of my neck. Six seconds. There is so
much noise. I sit forward and start to get up. Seven
seconds. I get to my feet and bump into the referee's
chest. Eight seconds. I look over the ref's right shoulder
to the corner where Eubank is standing. Nine seconds,
and then everybody hears the bell. Twenty-two thousand
people at White Hart Lane, twelve million watching on
TV in the comfort of their homes, and two boxers locked
in the middle of a most ferocious and brutal fight. I start
to shuffle instinctively back to my corner and then
Jimmy grabs me. Round Eleven is over and I have to
score it a draw.

The sixty-second break between Round Eleven and
Round Twelve: I sit down and push my gumshield out
like all fighters do at the end of the round. They start to
splash me with water. They never slap me. I tell Jimmy:
'I'm fine.' He keeps on peering into my eyes. 'I'm fine,
I'm fine,' I tell him again. I stand up when the bell
sounds and just remain in one spot. I say something
over my shoulder to Jimmy as he climbs out. I'm
talking, I'm fine. The referee calls for me to come to the
centre of the ring, but I stay in the same spot. Jimmy
thinks I'm playing for time but I don't know what I'm

thinking. I'm just stuck there and then the ref comes over to get me and grabs my arm to lead me to the centre of the ring.

Round Twelve: For the first time Eubank lands the first punch in a round. It hits my guard, and so does his next one. I'm backed into the corner and he falls into me trying to take me out. I'm covering up and moving my head back and away from his punches. One or two are getting through but just one or two. I'm not going down again, but I'm not throwing any punches back at him. He falls into me once more and puts my head in a powerful headlock. The referee separates us and he throws five or six more punches that I roll back and away from. It is no good, I'm not throwing any punches and Roy jumps in. The fight is over after just twenty-nine seconds of Round Twelve. Roy's arms are across my chest, his hair is flying all over the place in the breeze and I'm looking over his shoulder again. I have no idea what I'm looking at but I think it is Eubank. Yeah, I know somewhere deep inside my soul that I'm looking at Eubank. I'm not sure what is going through my mind, but I have a pretty good idea. It is over.

'That's it, son,' the referee tells me.

'Roy, no way, Roy. No way, Roy.' It is Jimmy screaming and Dean is at his side and they are chasing Roy all over the ring.

I'm now in Tim's arms back in my own corner, and people are

starting to jump into all parts of the ring. Roy is arguing with Jimmy and Dean.

'Jim, that's it. He's had enough,' he finally tells them.

The fight is over and I'm hidden behind and beneath men in tracksuits. I have seen the tapes that few have seen and watched the horror unfold. There is chaos and confusion and fights at ringside. I'm still in the corner somewhere. There is no commentary on the tape I watch, just the sound of silence and the increasing looks of fear and confusion on the faces of everybody still in the ring.

I watch as a briefcase is placed gently under my head, my face so gentle and serene. I have seen that kind act too many times, but I never watch beyond that point. I don't need to. I know what happened.

Chapter 8

Darkness.

The fight was over at 10.54 p.m. and five minutes later I started to die in the ring. It is that simple. I was placed on the bloodstained canvas in my corner when it was obvious that I could no longer stand on my own. The pressure inside my head was so severe that I soon collapsed, and I was in Tim's arms when the life started to fade from my body. The blood from a grazed left eye and a trickle from my nose left a stain on Tim's jacket. My white shorts were pink from the blood, but that was all just superficial blood. The real damage was inside my head where a small lump of blood was forming on the surface of my brain. I was getting closer and closer to death.

At 11.08 Jimmy, Kamel and Tim carried me out of the ring. We went out under the ropes at the exact same spot that Eubank had vaulted over about an hour earlier. The men carrying me staggered and nearly dropped me as they negotiated the steep drop from the canvas to the earth. I was actually passed over the heads of Radio Five's commentary team of Ian Darke and John Rawling.

My body was carried through a tunnel of security guards and the curious who had remained after the fight was over to savour the atmosphere. The men holding the stretcher's handles ran the gauntlet to get me off the pitch and into the main stadium as fast as possible. I was on my side and slowly fading away during this desperate race to get me from the ring to a hospital. It was a race for my life.

I was carried past Mum and the church brethren, Eric Seccombe and hundreds of other people I knew. I will never be able to imagine the horror and fear they experienced as my body hurtled past their eyes. Mum was told I was exhausted, others were told that a few minutes after leaving the ring I was sitting up drinking tea in the changing room. Both were lies. No one knew what the real situation was.

Before the men carrying me had left the pitch, the tannoy continued making announcements in the normal way. No one knew the gravity of the situation. It chilled me when I heard the announcements as I watched the tapes.

The clock was ticking incredibly fast against me by the time I was placed in the back of an ambulance. I know now that there is a 'golden hour' for people with head injuries. I was running deep into the hour by the time I was on my way to the first hospital. Tim and the British Boxing Board of Control's doctor, Stephan Shapiro, were with me in the back. The North

Middlesex hospital is just a short drive away and on a Saturday night its emergency ward would have been busy with people waiting to be seen.

My ambulance arrived at the North Middlesex at 11.22. I know from my medical records that I had stopped breathing properly before arriving at the hospital. In other words I had died either in the ambulance or during the frantic rush from the ring. I had stopped breathing. It is a thought I can barely comprehend.

The deterioration of my condition had been steady from the end of the fight up until the point that I arrived at the hospital, where thankfully they were able to resuscitate me. My pupils were fixed and dilated, and my brain stem had suffered an injury. After I was resuscitated, one pupil had unfixed and my life was extended for another few minutes or hours. As the court later found, the main problem was that I had been taken to a hospital without the facilities to operate on me and save my life.

When I looked at the medical notes I found out that by the time they got me to the North Middlesex there was insufficient breath to sustain life and my life was nearly over. The simple way to start the life-saving process is to put a tube down the person's throat and blow oxygen into the lungs. That is what happened, and it saved me. A brain scan was taken, and of course it revealed the clot, and then the unimaginable journey continued on that long night. The reason people die from blood clots is because they are denied oxygen. At the North Middlesex that night they reversed the process and kept me alive, kept me fighting, but there was only so much they could do. I had to be taken somewhere where they could operate.

In a room at the hospital Mum and Uncle Joe, surrounded by members from the church, held a prayer meeting. I was twenty feet away, in an open ward, and I still had my white boxing boots on. Nurses hovered at the end of my bed, and one or two close friends came by to look on helplessly. Some members of the press had arrived, but they thankfully showed some restraint and respect and waited on the edge. There were drunks, exhausted nurses and weary doctors all around, and in the middle of this crazy situation a doctor and a nurse, whose Saturday night shift had just taken a hellish diversion, were keeping me alive.

At 11.55, about thirty minutes after arriving, I was put back in an ambulance and a doctor and a nurse joined me in the cramped space. The blood clot was pressing on my brain and the second leg of the race to save my life started with the sirens flashing as the ambulance left the North Middlesex for the drive to St Bartholomew's hospital. A car packed with friends left the hospital, and behind that Mum and Uncle Joe joined the cavalcade. The journalists were also on their way.

Back at White Hart Lane the news was spreading fast that the situation was extremely serious. The press at the fight were in touch with their newsrooms, and an army of midnight reporters, cameramen and photographers were being mobilised to lay siege to Bart's long before I arrived there.

The team at Bart's led by the senior registrar, George Stephenson were ready for my arrival and started the vital balls rolling during the early critical moments until the consultant neuro-surgeon, Peter Hamlyn, could make his way in from home. He had been having a quiet Saturday night when he was contacted by his department and warned that a man was coming in having sustained an injury in 'a fight'. He was asked if he would also help with the press.

'What press?' Peter had asked.

'The press are downstairs and it looks like there are hundreds of them,' he was told.

He had no idea what to expect, but as soon as his cab pulled up near the front of the hospital he realised that something very special had happened and the figure had not been an exaggeration. The front door was surrounded: the ornate arches that form the front of the Victorian hospital were packed with broadcasters and other members of the media. He told the driver to go round the back in the hope that he would be able to find an open door or find somebody to open a door for him. He wondered what had happened to the bag lady that lived in one of the arched doorways near the main entrance. She had been there for a long time and he knew that each morning the nurses took her a cup of tea. He told me that he thought of her at that moment and hoped that all the people had not forced her out on to the street.

It was probably close to one in the morning and it was the beginning of what Peter calls his 'lost weekend'. At the rear of the hospital he knew of one door that would give him immediate access to the stairs that led up to the operating rooms, but he also knew that for obvious security reasons the door would be firmly locked from the inside. Peter walked as calmly and quickly as he could and reached the door without anybody spotting him. As he expected, the door was locked. He had a crisis on his hands because he realised that time was running out for the man upstairs being prepared for an emergency operation. He contemplated running to the front and pushing his way past the crowd that was hanging about there.

He tapped the door once more, possibly in frustration at the ridiculous situation that he was in, and it suddenly opened. It was a miracle, and then he saw that the bag lady was standing there. She said not a word, and he took off, running up the stairs to the operating theatre. The role that the old woman played in my life will never be fully known, but if nobody had heard Peter knocking on that door, his arrival in the operating theatre could have been severely delayed. I always add the bag lady of Bart's to my list of saviours, many of whom, just like her, remain anonymous to this day.

By the time I was examined at Bart's, the blood clot was the size of a saucer of milk and at that time there was nothing in my brain working. My pupils were dilated and I needed to be ventilated and operated on as soon as possible. I was scanned and then taken up to theatre for the first of six major operations on my brain. I was prepared for surgery and wheeled in shortly before 1 a.m. on Sunday 22 September, 1991.

I have been told there was a great sense of anticipation in the theatre that morning when I was wheeled in. Peter quickly realised that I was not just a man with an injury from any old fight. He was well aware of the previous evening's championship encounter. He knew Eubank, he knew me, and as he prepared his hands and then looked down at my skull, he was ready to perform his third operation on a boxer with a blood clot. His previous two patients, Rod Douglas in 1989 and Robert Darko in 1990, had both survived. It is doubtful if there is a neurosurgeon anywhere in the world who has performed live-saving operations on more boxers than Peter Hamlyn. At a few minutes after 1 a.m. he was ready to add me to his list of survivors.

In the operating theatre there were two surgeons, two nurses and two anaesthetists. There were also an operating department attendant and a couple of runners. The operation started with a big insertion in my scalp, and then the skin was pulled back off my skull. A motorised saw was then used to cut through the exposed skull, and that revealed the size of the blood clot. The clot was sucked away and the piece of skull, or bone flap as it is also known, was put back on again. The first operation took ninety minutes.

Peter's neurological team worked perfectly together. The operation was over before three in the morning and the pressure was off my brain, but it was only a temporary reprieve. I don't think anybody in that theatre believed it would be that simple, quick and easy. I had suffered too much from the moment Roy Francis put his arms across my chest until the moment the scalpel cut smoothly through my skin.

I was prepared for the Intensive Care Unit and at 4.20 in the morning I had my first visitors – Mum and Uncle Joe were allowed to see me. My solicitor, Henri Brandman, was also with them. Mum recoiled when she saw the size of the bandage on my head and the tubes that were coming in and out of me. She could not take her eyes off one tube that was coming from behind my head and was full of blood. She cried the first of a million tears at my bedside. She had seen it before when Jeff had been rushed to hospital as a baby. That night at the ICU in Bart's, she had to look at her eldest son and understand that, just like with Jeff all those years earlier, she could lose him.

I was as still as a statue; only the gentle humming of the intensive care unit's machines disturbed the silence. She took my hand and touched my skin for the first time since leaving the house in Chingford the day before. She had been smiling when she had said goodbye the day before, but as she held my hand in the early hours of that morning there was no joy in her face. Once again, one of her sons was being kept alive by a machine. Peter was honest with her. He thought I could die, and that my recovery, if there was to be any, would be slow. Mum returned to the hospital's waiting area where my family, close friends and members of the church had gathered. A friend of mine told me that my mum aged ten years in the twenty minutes she was upstairs with me. She thought I was going to die, because that is what the experts thought.

At 5.10 Jimmy Tibbs was sent for, and he briefly saw me in a meeting that stretched his belief and faith in God. Jimmy prayed by my bed that night for the first time, and I know that he was in turmoil. Some people had pointed the finger at him for letting me go out for Round Twelve. 'It's my fault, I should never have let you go out,' he once told me. 'No, Jim, that's not right. Nobody is to blame,' I had to tell him, but on that first visit there were no words that I could say to ease his troubled heart.

When Jimmy came down, he knelt and prayed with Mum, Uncle Joe and some of the church brethren. Eric Seccombe was there, as was Jon Robinson and Jimmy's son, Mark. They all prayed for a miracle.

At 6.05 Peter came down to make a statement, and was quickly surrounded by reporters and cameramen. He made it to one side, next to the admissions desk and just out of earshot of Mum and my friends.

He looked exhausted, totally drained, and at first the press were convinced he had arrived to announce my death. To great relief, his first statement was not a death notice, but it was bleak. However, I was still alive against all the odds.

'Essentially Michael has suffered a severe injury and has undergone some emergency surgical treatment to the back of the head and is at the moment on the intensive care unit.

'He is obviously in a quite critical state, though at the moment he is stable. We will continue to give him all the treatment we can and I'm hopeful that we will be able to make some progress.

'But I can make no real definitive statement about his prognosis or likely outcome at the moment.'

That was it – living, but just. The biggest fight had, to borrow one of Peter's words, entered a critical stage.

*

At some point that morning my mum left the hospital and went back to my house in Chingford. The police had to go and get her late in the afternoon when I was once again close to death, possibly closer than I had ever been, and was being prepared for more emergency brain surgery.

I had been in the intensive care unit for less than twelve hours when the pressure in my skull threatened my life once again. I was under constant observation in the ICU, where teams of three watched over each of the patients, and it was clear that I needed to go back to theatre. There had been more bleeding and I needed more surgery or I would die.

Many years later Peter told me that he was out having a late lunch with his mother and father and wife in central London on that Sunday afternoon. He had been up all night saving me, and after a brief sleep back at his flat he had got up to find the Sunday papers full of stories and tragic pictures of the boxer he had operated on. His parents were proud of their son, but they were not very impressed when his pager went off at the dining table in the restaurant. He had to leave and get back to Bart's and the same operating theatre he had left earlier that morning.

The pressure was mounting when Peter and his team went back inside my head on that Sunday afternoon. They scraped away the blood and did their best to stabilise me, but by now they were increasingly concerned, not just about my survival, but about the quality of life I would have if I did survive. This was a grim topic for the people in the operating theatre to consider. Peter had to speak with Mum and Uncle Joe again to keep them fully up to date, and at the same time make them brutally aware of just how seriously hurt I was and how seriously damaged I could be if I did come through.

I have been told since that a patient in a head trauma situation either bounces back or dies. I was dragging out the process, and Peter admits I was going into territory he had never been in before and has never been in since. He had expected one or two critical moments, but I was at the start of an almost daily round of emergencies that went on and on.

After surgery that afternoon, Peter decided to leave out the piece of skull that he had removed during the first operation to get at the surface of my brain. When he had finished the first operation he had put the piece back, but that afternoon the threat and danger to my life was so serious that he did not want to close my head for fear of the pressure mounting and killing me. Not putting the piece of skull back in place meant that if the swelling returned it could bulge out through the hole in my head. If there was sudden activity I would not be in immediate danger because the surgeons would gain some extra time. It shows just close to the edge I was, and also that every second would be crucial if I had to be rushed once more from the ICU to the operating theatre.

A bandage was placed round my head and I was wheeled back to the ICU for the next round in my struggle. Before I left the theatre, Peter walked over, took a black marker pen from a shelf and wrote three words on the bandage. The words remained on my dressing for a very long time and they shocked a lot of my visitors. 'No bone flap'.

Back in the ICU the non-stop monitoring continued and I

returned to my still existence. A long way from the machines the boxing world carried on without my involvement, and at seven o'clock that night over a thousand people took their seats at the Grosvenor House Hotel for the Muhammad Ali function. The talk, as was to be expected, was all about my condition, and Jimmy and Jon were in demand. On Jon's table there was an empty seat between him and Jimmy and the pair soon grew tired of turning people away. Some of my other friends were on the table and the event clearly helped take their mind off the fight and the fallout of the previous twenty-four hours. It was not until about eight o'clock that it was revealed that Ali was not going to show, which was a fitting end to a weekend of drama in the boxing business – on the Friday Frank Bruno had been granted a licence to return to the ring after a thirty-month gap, on the Saturday was my fight, and on the Sunday Ali went missing from his own testimonial.

Mum was still at my bedside on the Sunday night when I had a surprise visitor, the one person I would have least expected to show up at that time. At some point during the early evening a slight woman in a headscarf arrived at the ICU and asked to see me. At first the protective nurses tried to turn her away, but then Mum spotted her and led her into the ICU, where the eerie blue light and the machines created a calm feeling. It was Zara. She stayed that night after Mum left and was joined at my bedside by Ambrose Mendy. Later that same evening another close friend of mine arrived after leaving the Ali function early, and the trio stood there praying, touching my hands and crying silently.

Zara was gone by Tuesday, which was the day the *Sun* published a front-page picture of her looking from a window in one of the many waiting rooms. That same day my girlfriend replaced Zara at my bedside. She had stayed away out of respect for me on the first two nights until she knew that Zara had left. There was no squabble over my body in the ICU between the women in my life. One was the mother of my children and the other was my girlfriend. They were worried about me, not each other.

Downstairs, the press horde had formed a makeshift camp that made it virtually impossible for anybody even remotely connected to me to come and see me without being pestered. There was a secret tunnel that allowed people to enter without detection, and some of my more high-profile visitors came to my bed that way. The nurses at the door of the ICU were fierce in the protection of their patients and nobody, no matter how famous, got in unless Mum or one of my close friends agreed. A lot of my friends had to open their bags to prove that there were no hidden cameras or tape recorders inside them.

The drama went on for days. I once asked Peter about the first few days and the early problems. I can remember him stopping what he was doing and looking at me, laughing.

'Michael,' he told me, 'it was not days. You were on a knife-edge for two months.'

He told me about the thirty people I met in a two- or three-hour period after the fight that I had never seen before, all of whom played a part in my survival after Eubank's last punches, and that includes the bag lady. I owe my life to all of them. I don't even know most of their names, but then again they never knew me before I came into their lives for a brief and shocking period that weekend. I was just an unconscious man in a bad state and they acted together to save me.

A person in an ICU with a serious head injury is hanging in the balance between survival or death, and the signs, good and bad, are there from the very start. During the first week there were many occasions when Peter prepared my mother for my death, but he never actually said I would die and he never told her to go and say 'Goodbye'. These are two myths. However, he did let her know in very strong language that I could die at any time.

Peter has never met anybody who hovered so close to death and yet survived like I did. I always tell him that I was destined to survive and that he worried about me for nothing. It was, I know from my medical records, an increasingly hopeless prospect, and he and a lot of people were convinced I would die. Each day was a miracle, and one day at a time was as much as anybody could hope or plan for. I know it was the spirit of God that was giving me strength to defy all the experts.

On the Tuesday after the fight, Eubank came to see me. He took advantage of the secret tunnel and arrived very late at night when nobody else was visiting. In the small and extremely personal waiting room, where there were a few beds for exhausted relatives, Eubank and Mum met and talked. She told him that she had nothing to forgive him for, but he was extremely low and full of guilt.

I was a particularly disturbing sight during the first weeks because leading up to the fight I had been in the best physical shape of my career – so many people have told me how good I looked. Though I had tubes coming in and out of me and I was connected to all the machines, my chest down to my waist was exposed – and I was in great condition. The muscle definition on my arms was tremendous and even the small bruises and grazes on my face faded fast. I looked peaceful and almost healthy, and it was too much for some people.

Of course my appearance was deceptive, because my every breath was false, the work of a machine that was breathing for me and keeping me alive.

Peter and the other doctors looked for signs of increased life each and every day for a month, but still the ventilator had to keep pounding the breath in and out of my body. The most basic parts of my brain, the bits that make a person breathe in and out, were not working. During the first month there was no sign that that crucial piece of brain would ever function again.

Each night Mum would wait at my bedside until the very last moment before leaving and going to a small room that had been found for her to sleep in, so that she could stay at the hospital and not have to travel back and forward. She would lock the door, pray, and then settle down for a night of sleep that she hoped would not be interrupted by a nurse knocking on the door and telling her to come upstairs because of an emergency. There were many nights when someone did and they were terrible for her to have to endure.

Peter told her that I would more than likely have appalling disabilities if I survived. She was told I would probably be in a permanent vegetative state. I cannot even begin to imagine how I would respond to being told something like that. Mum, I know, turned to prayer and her belief in the Lord.

I once asked Peter how he found the strength to tell parents that their children would possibly die or be seriously disabled. He just shrugged and said that it came with the territory and that it was never pleasant. He also admitted that there were many times during that first long month when he questioned what he was doing, asked whether it was really worth it and, more importantly, whether I would thank him in the end.

'You thought I was going to be a vegetable?' I asked him.

He nodded.

Peter and the others at Bart's have to deal with a lot of seemingly impossible situations on an almost daily basis. It is never easy, but perhaps the hardest part of all is that they have to provide answers to questions that are impossible to answer. I know there were days, possibly even weeks, when the team led by Peter had to ask themselves, would I really want to be back with such serious injuries? Also, and I know this must have been hard to answer, did *they* really want me back in the state they were predicting? But they kept up their expert and devoted vigil, accompanied by their endless hope, and watched every bleep on the machine that monitored my life and at the same time gave me life.

There was a theoretical possibility that I would survive and make a recovery, but, according to Peter and the experts, I would still be 'fantastically disturbed'. I felt a shiver go down my spine one day a few years ago when I heard that expression for the first time. What is painfully clear from the first month when I was deep in a coma is that nobody expected me to have much of a life. Mum prayed, my friends prayed and everybody wanted a miracle, but the doctors were in possession of the facts.

During the long days and lonely nights of the first month, Mum would often be joined in her room by one or two of the women from the Evering church. Sister Lynne was a constant source of spiritual support, and she and the others had the ability to cheer up Peter, even when he delivered bad news. Peter would arrive at Mum's little bedroom with a further complication and a reminder that the prognosis was bleak, but always left feeling a bit lighter, he admits. There was tremendous faith in that room, and it touched more than a few people at Bart's during my long stay.

For the first weeks my girls were not allowed to see me. I am glad they were kept away. It would have been too distressing for them. I remained on a knife-edge for a month before there were any positive signs of recovery. The hospital issued statements, the press continued to wait and the world outside my darkness continued without me.

In the end it was hope and faith and belief that helped me survive the first weeks. As the first month came to an end there were certain small signs that everybody at my bedside found encouraging. Mum would stand for hours rubbing my hand and gently singing to me. She was a popular and positive presence in the ICU at Bart's.

It was considered an improvement if I blinked or moved an eyebrow or my right side responded in some way. Peter and his people had started to detect increased neurological movement and at the end of the month I could help myself breathe with the assistance of the tracheotomy tube that was in my throat. But there were still a lot of scary moments when I required the full attention of all the emergency staff at the ICU.

Absolutely any sign of independent life was a celebration at this most crucial and critical of times. I was working alongside the life support machine by now – I was no longer 100 per cent dependent on it to live. It was not much, but it was a definite sign that I was coming back and getting stronger against the odds.

Between the end of October and Christmas I started to do more things. Nobody knows for certain when I first opened my eyes or first responded to a question, but my mum told me that she kept asking me to squeeze her hand, and that one day I did! But once I started to come back from the darkness there was no stopping me. I was starting to recognise people at this time.

I moved my right hand, I opened my eyes and I responded with blinks to questions each day from early November. By the middle of November I was moved from the ICU to a recovery ward called the W. G. Grace, which was often a very frightening place to be. I know a lot of people died in that ward during my stay and, unlike the ICU, it was noisy. People have told me that visiting me in the ICU was peaceful but that visits to the Grace ward were always frantic.

This was the start of my gruelling recovery, and the months

and months when I was trapped and silent and desperate for a faster journey from the darkness. I would stare at the ceiling. The days and nights could be long and painful. I prayed for use of my body, I asked God to bring back my body. I was in a terrible and frustrating prison. I felt completely isolated and trapped.

During my first month in hospital I had lost a stone in weight and I needed to get my strength up again. I had physiotherapists to help restore my wasted and wasting muscles. It was a slow process and became very, very painful. I responded well to all sorts of physiotherapy that I was having, and the stimulation was helping, but I remained locked inside my still body.

Peter still remained cautious about my recovery, but he complimented Mum on her defiance and refusal to give in. I happen to know that he could not believe what was happening to me. But I had unbelievable faith and that is what I had to fight back with. I have told him many, many times since then that I was saved for a reason.

In November a friend arrived with *Boxing Monthly*. Another friend at the bedside noticed what she thought were clear signs of recognition from me as the pages were turned. The man who had brought the magazine was reading me the articles and talking to me about boxing. I was not a boxer that ignored the sport, I was a boxer that loved the sport, and I loved the company and friendship of fellow fighters. As my friend was reading me fight reports and talking to me in general about the scene, my other friend suddenly came over to the side of the bed.

'Michael, touch the picture of Mike Tyson,' she asked me.

I moved my right hand a few inches and tapped Tyson's head. My friends were very excited because nobody believed that I was capable of doing such a thing at that stage of my recovery. I had moved my hand, understood the question and carried out a task. My friends were stunned and excited. They were also sensible enough to know that it could have been a fluke, an involuntary reaction.

'OK, Michael, touch Evander Holyfield,' she continued.

I did it again and I was correct.

'That's too easy because it's just one picture on one page and we're holding the page under his fingers,' the man with the magazine said.

They opened the magazine and found two pages where there were eight pictures and not all of the fighters were well known. They moved the pages to within a few inches of my right hand.

'Michael, touch Duke McKenzie,' she said.

No problem, I touched Duke's head. My two friends were nearly jumping into each other's arms.

'Perhaps that was just luck,' the man said.

'OK, Michael, touch Kirkland Laing,' she asked.

Without a pause I moved my finger to the highest corner of the page and tapped my old friend Kirk on his head. I had done it, I had obeyed commands, followed instructions and pulled off a mini-miracle. I had done it again and again. It was surely a great day in my recovery, a moment when we all felt blessed. At that point in my treatment it was thought that recognition and response was just an occasional occurrence, but the test with the *Boxing Monthly* had shown that it was not random – I had been asked specific questions and I had answered correctly time after time.

I began to do more and more each day, and was allowed to sit up higher and higher each day in the special bed. At some point in late November or early December my two little girls were allowed to come up and see their daddy. The curtains were pulled together and I had some privacy to sit with my girls. They had made drawings for me, and these were fixed over my bed with all the others that had been coming in since I had been admitted.

With my two little girls inside my tented area I'm sure I felt very happy. Mum and one or two close friends were there. I know I just sat there, and I have been told that I looked, for the first time since the fight, content. I'm sure I did, because I can't think of anything that would have pleased me more. I was alive, and I had my girls at my side, even though I could not talk to them or hug them.

The girls were allowed to come a few more times to the W. G. Grace ward, and of course there were a lot of other visitors.

Christmas came and went, and after the festivities there was talk of the next stop on my journey. I was going to be moved to Homerton hospital's special rehabilitation unit. I knew that area well – it is contained on the same two pages in the London A–Z as most of the rest of my life. I was due to move in January 1992 for what would be the 'hardest' part of my comeback. I had no idea then, but what I was going to be made to suffer and endure at Homerton was not going to be the hardest or the lowest point in my recovery. It was physically draining and painful at Homerton, but I had years of struggling to come after that.

But for the moment the fight continued and it looked like I was just staying in front. I had survived for a reason – it was God's will. I had a lot of work to do before I would get my body and mind back, but I was on my way, and with God's help and the support of those around me I knew I would get there. The biggest fight was well and truly underway.

Chapter 9

There are several years in my life when I was not in the spotlight and was a long way from the attention of the public. Obviously, when I was a child nobody knew me, then when I first turned professional Mickey Duff wanted me kept a secret, and then there was the twelve-month period from the end of January 1992 until the end of January 1993. It was a time that required incredible faith, through which, thankfully, I was able to survive the darkest days of my life.

I was transferred from Bart's at the end of January 1992, just four months after I had been rushed in unconscious and close to death. I went out in another ambulance, and this time my eyes were open, but I saw little and remembered nothing. I was going to an unknown future trapped in silence and would soon have just walls and bricks to look at.

A few days before I left, Peter Hamlyn was quoted in the

Daily Telegraph of 16 January. He mentioned that the tracheotomy tube had been removed from my throat. With the tube gone, I was breathing on my own and had the chance to speak again. Peter put my recovery into brutal perspective. I still have the cutting and occasionally I like to look at it and dozens of others that made equally grim forecasts.

Peter was quoted as saying, 'It has clearly been disappointing to me and to his family that he isn't better. That was due to the delay in resuscitation time.'

Peter later gave evidence in the court case and went on to recommend more safety measures to complement the eight proposals that were introduced by the British Boxing Board of Control just six weeks after my last fight. The first one of the Board's new ideas was particularly relevant to me, which made it disturbing for me to read: 'The accident, emergency and neurological units of the hospital nearest to the venue to be preadvised.'

I knew then that the doctors and staff at the North Middlesex had been inadequately prepared for my arrival. I had landed in their busy emergency room in the middle of a typical Saturday night for the staff of the midnight shift. But more importantly, there was not a neurological unit at the North Middlesex. Put simply, I had gone to the wrong hospital and lost time in the backs of ambulances – and the time I lost nearly cost me my life. If the Board's rulings had been in place, I would never have been in the North Middlesex that night, I would have been elsewhere and under the surgeon's knife a lot sooner.

The most important of the eight points was number three.

Peter had constantly made the point about the need for urgent resuscitation at ringside, preferably by one of the 50,000 trained anaesthetists in Britain. Number three on the Board's list dealt with this inadequacy and recommended that, 'Full and adequate resuscitation equipment is available at ringside supervised by fully trained staff.'

My injuries were the result of a deficiency in the systems in place. I had not been resuscitated and now my prognosis, as Peter said in the *Daily Telegraph*, was not good: 'As I said in the early days after Michael's injury, he will be lucky to be entirely normal, but he'll be unlucky now if he succumbs to his injuries.'

I was living, getting better, but there was still a chance that my injury could take my life. If that happened it would be, so Peter said, 'unlucky', but it could still possibly happen. I would sit and think about the word 'unlucky' and wonder just how much unluckier I could be.

Homerton Hospital was a dreary place. The hospital's rehabilitation unit was an old building in the middle of the main building, which was even older. The Victorian unit has been pulled down.

The hospital was on the edge of Hackney. I knew the area well. There was a boxing gym in one of the nearby council estates and I had sparred there on a few occasions. Had I been able to get up from my bed, I could have walked to all of the important places of my early life.

First stop would have been the spot where the car hit the pram and knocked Jeff and me across the street. A few minutes from the zebra crossing that Mum was crossing was the house in

Rectory Road where the fire had started. A few hundred metres from the scene of the inferno was the flat in Forest Road where we had lived after leaving Uncle Joe's house. At the end of Forest Road was my first primary school, Queensbridge. I could have covered all of the sites in a fifteen-minute walk from where my bed was. Instead I was stuck, trapped flat on my back most of the time and forced to watch the world drift slowly by.

I know that I was relatively unaware of my surroundings when I first arrived on the old ward. I know I was in a dazed and often confused state, because Dr Richard Greenwood, the consultant neurologist in charge of the unit, has told me several times. He recognised in me all the usual problems, but he was instantly struck by my determination, as were all of the specialists who started to pull my body and mind to bits. At Bart's they had been focused on saving my life, but at Homerton they were determined to give me as much of my life back as they could.

At Bart's I had responded to all types of therapy, but I was unprepared for the intensity of my routine at the new place. It caught me off guard and it shocked and stunned a lot of my friends, who often watched in horror as my body was being forced to change. Some have told me that they had to look away when it was obvious that I was in pain, when yet another woman pushed one of my limbs into another painful position.

Mum also suffered during the early days at Homerton because she was having flashbacks to when she had performed similar stretching and pulling exercises with Jeff after his injury. I never cease to be amazed by the mental strength and depth of faith in my mother and how it kept her going in the face of such relentless adversity in her life. At Homerton she once again had to start looking after one of her sons as if he was a little baby and begin from scratch.

In the first dark and silent year, success was measured in centimetres by the physiotherapists. They tugged and dragged my body back from the very edge and treated me like I had done something wrong. They would explain to me, as I sat and eyed them from my distant world, that they were going to work on my left side or my right side, and then they would go about torturing me. They had to work the muscles on both legs and try and bring the shrinking left side back. The right side was getting stronger and stronger under their expert hands, but the left was lame and needed more persuasion.

The complete lack of recovery on my left side was exactly what Peter had feared from the very start. The brain injury I suffered had left me immobile down that side, which was always called 'his paralysed side' whenever people talked about me. Nothing down that side of my body was working or responding, but still they pulled and pulled. I kept faith in my own ability to get better, and I had equal faith in the hands of the woman in charge of making better. But it was a very long and very painful process.

It was a relief some nights to go back to my bed and have Mum comb my hair as I watched a video. In Homerton I watched a lot of action movies, and I'm told that most were particularly violent. One night I watched a tape of the Eubank rematch in Homerton and I wish that somebody had filmed me watching it. I'm still never sure how to distinguish what I remember from that night from what I remember from watching it hundreds of times on video.

I was used to physical training – after all I had trained for most of my life – but the physiotherapy was something else. Sadly, I never had the voice to shout out and tell them to leave me alone. But I realise now that every night I went to bed aching was a good night, because I was feeling something.

The months went by and in early May I was being put through my paces once again by Annie Meharg, the wonderful woman in charge of my necessary torture. It was a normal session and then something truly amazing happened. She had one of my legs in her hands and she was bending it all over the place, just like she had done hundreds of times, and I was making the same faces that I had made hundreds of times, and the pain was clearly more than unbearable because for the first time since the end of Round Eleven, nearly eight months earlier I spoke a word. Actually, I screamed out in agony.

'ANNIE!'

It was what a lot of people had been waiting to hear, and from that point on the physiotherapy became a bit easier and I started to put more and more words together. I was hard to understand, and my voice, when I was not screaming in agony, was very low. But I was fighting back, and I could tell that everybody working on my body and head was impressed. I'm just glad I got those five letters out when I did. I'm not sure how much more silent agony I could have put up with.

Before I started to speak I had to use a rotary board to

communicate with Jill Dawson, the occupational therapist, during our sessions. They realised quickly that I had not forgotten my ABC or how to count. Jill was the one who taught me how to brush my teeth again and to put my arm back in a shirt. I was a child once more, a baby really, and that is why Mum always claims it was harder for me to come back from my injury than it was for Jeff. He was just a baby, still in nappies, when he was injured. I was a grown man, and somewhere deep inside my brain I knew that once upon a time I had brushed my own teeth and pulled my own socks on.

Annie worked on getting my body ready for the normal things I had once done, and Jill reminded me to do the things that I had long stopped doing. The process took a year before there were any major signs of improvement, but each day Annie and Jill and the other therapists left my side happy in the knowledge that my rehabilitation had moved in the right direction just a little bit more.

That year when I vanished off the face of the earth it was probably a good thing, because there is nothing remotely glamorous about a neurological recovery unit. It is a life of endless personal suffering. But it is counterbalanced by daily contact with some of the most fabulous individuals that anybody could ever meet. I could never name all of them – I don't know all their names – but they are remembered in my heart. I can clearly recall one woman forever going on in a good-natured way that my stomach muscles were too good. She struggled with me for over a year to give me some flexibility and I only found out a few years ago that her name was Cherry Kilbride. I met her again one day on a return trip to Homerton in 1999 for a summer fête. She came over to speak to me.

'Michael, do you remember me?' she asked.

'Just fill me in on who you are,' I asked her.

'I was the one giving you the therapy from the start,' she told me.

Cherry had worked on me when I was still in Bart's. I hope she wasn't too disappointed that I failed to recognise her, but, sadly, over the years I have forgotten hundreds of people.

From the first moment in the day until the lights went out, the different sessions were all designed to add to the recovery. There are no miracles in rehab, just like there are not meant to be miracles in surgery, but miracles do happen. I know that.

One happened on 27 May 1992 when I was moved back to Bart's to finally have my head closed. I was due to go back into surgery with Peter so that he could fix a titanium plate in my skull. It sounds scary, but we all considered it routine and just a necessary addition to my slow-moving recovery.

I'm sure that being back in Bart's was odd, if not for me then for my supporters, because in the four months that I had been at Homerton I had done a lot of work and made considerable progress in all areas. I knew that Peter was happy with the way his special patient was responding.

One day I was in the ward waiting for the operation when I sensed a disturbance in the hall, and a few seconds later the door opened and a man walked in. A close friend of mine, who was sitting next to me, said that my eyes widened and then I smiled – she said it was the first smile she had seen on my face since before the fight. I had good reason to smile, because at the end of my bed was the man known as 'The Greatest': Muhammad Ali. *He* had come to see *me*. My mum and Uncle Joe were at his side and he was smiling. He came close to my ear and spoke.

'Boy, you're pretty, but I'm prettier than you,' he said to me.

At that point there were several witnesses to a second smile on my face, and then I raised my right hand higher than I had lifted it since the fight and touched fists with my idol. There were gasps round the room, and Peter could hardly believe his eyes. He had watched me leave four months earlier, barely able to blink and move my hand an inch, and here I was back under his care, smiling and giving high-fives with the greatest sportsman in history. It was an overwhelming moment. Nobody had ever expected this much to happen.

Ali's visit was a breakthrough for me. I felt happy and honoured.

The visit from Ali was particularly memorable for Mum because she had always been a great fan of his. She posed for pictures with him, and before Ali left he joked with a few of the people in the ward. Ali's voice was so low that he could only make himself heard if he spoke directly into your ear. He went over to Leroy Meggi, who is a big solid man, and with a mischievous grin on his face he said a few words. Leroy started to laugh and later told us all what Ali had said to him: 'Boy, you look like Joe Frazier.' Ali had called Frazier some horrific things in the build-up to their three fights and most of the insults revolved around Frazier's supposed ugliness. But Leroy was not bothered in the slightest.

That day was a tremendous boost, and the only time in a bleak year when anything different or memorable happened. I was soon back in Homerton with the titanium plate in my skull, and as soon as I had recovered enough from the operation, the fight for my health continued.

When I first went to Homerton I would spend time in the standing frame, which helped to stretch muscles that had started to decline. Because of my size, and because I was totally unable to support myself in any way, it had required five or six people to get me standing in the frame. I had no control over my body and I was starting to put on weight, which was quite disturbing. At one point after the operation, when I was in a deep coma, I had dipped below eleven stone, but at Homerton I was fast approaching thirteen. I had to start watching my food or I would have even greater difficulty gaining control of my muscles because of the extra bulk.

It was because I was still unable to do very much that I was gaining weight and having trouble shifting it. I have always had a sweet tooth and even now I need to be careful about what I eat, especially if I get my meal times in a muddle. During the first six months at Homerton it was so important that I stayed on course for my amazing recovery that I had to resist the food that Mum delivered each day, even though I had no other comforts. She started to ration my portions, and it worked because everybody involved with my welfare could see some results by the end of the year. I could not help the women stretch my muscles, but

I could help everybody by watching my weight. It was just a small sign of my determination.

There was talk of me being allowed home for Christmas, and after Christmas being allowed home at weekends. It gave me something to look forward to, but during the start of the winter months of 1992, each and every day was an exhausting chore and my emotions went up and down. I still could not speak very well, I had no chance of walking, it took three people to hold me up in the standing frame and I viewed life from a sitting position. I needed somebody to feed me, wash me and clean me after I had used the toilet. I was thankful that I had survived the injury and the emergency surgery, but I was finding it increasingly difficult to tolerate the slow and deliberate pace of my rehabilitation.

Mum had told me when I first arrived at Homerton that she was dreading the process of recovery.

'You will need all your faith to get through this,' she had warned me.

By Christmas I was hitting rock bottom, or so I thought, until I got the news that I would definitely be able to spend the holidays in my house in Chingford.

Michael Watson was going home. And he had a wheelchair as a Christmas present.

I knew the street and I knew the house. I have forgotten now exactly what else was familiar to me, but I was slowly starting to remember more and more about my life. I was amazing people all of the time by nodding or pointing or reluctantly pushing out words. Being home for Christmas meant a ten-day break from the ward at Homerton, a break from my own private prison, where my isolation and frustration was often unbearable.

The ward was often difficult at night because a lot of people in there were suffering, and the cries and moans would go on for hours. I prayed for all of the people that were recovering with me at Homerton. Spending Christmas in my own home in Chingford I would enjoy the silence. I would also be with friends and family.

The previous Christmas at Bart's, on the W. G. Grace ward, I had sat and endured an endless stream of well-wishers at a time when I was really feeling antisocial. My friends could tell that I was not happy with all the visitors, but there was nothing I could do but sit in the bed and blink in answer to their questions. I spent that time praying for the ability to walk and talk. I could not feel my feet or hands, and I would pray for them to return to me. I wanted my body back, and I begged God to grant my wish. Fear and discouragement are not part of my system but the nights and days in recovery were very hard and very bleak. It was my faith that kept me going.

The *Daily Mirror* had launched a Michael Watson Appeal Fund, and during the Christmas period money arrived, often with cards from school children. There was one celebrity card the *Daily Mirror* organised that was signed by hundreds of well-known people. It went above my bed, next to a card from my old primary school, Whitmore. I also received a rosary from the Pope.

At my house, the downstairs living area was converted into my bedroom, and other adaptations made in order to accommodate my personal needs. I was surrounded by loving family and caring people so the indignities were not too much to bear. Besides, all that mattered was that I was home. Mum had worked in care homes, and my close friends were already familiar with a lot of my routines from their visits to Homerton.

I saw my girls but it was not easy because of my condition. The girls did finally come over and spend some time with me at Christmas. I can't remember what I gave them that year, as it is like a million other memories that have gone missing somewhere inside my head. Thankfully, I'm still recovering memories that I thought were gone.

I do know that this time they were far more inquisitive about their daddy's condition. In the hospital they had sat and watched and smiled, but in my house they wanted some answers. Jamilla was nearly six and Layla was four and they were both bright little girls. I loved them deeply, and that is why it hurt so much when they looked at me strangely.

'Daddy, why can't you walk?' Jamilla would ask, and then add, 'Daddy, what's wrong with your voice?'

In one of the earliest and clearest memories that I have, and one that has stayed with me when so many have been lost, is being in bed at night, and I make a promise that nobody will ever look at me with pity. I know that the bed was in Homerton, so I guess it happened in 1993. I didn't want my daughters, my family, my friends or strangers to see me differently. I wanted to be the same old Michael when they looked at me.

The Christmas was uneventful. Even though I had a wheel-chair, I never went out of the door. I spent the time inside, and a lot of the time I was sleeping because the medication that I was on made me drowsy. My speech was slow not just because my tongue was heavy, but because I was tired.

When I went back to Homerton in early January 1993 I was given a motorised wheelchair, and my life changed for the better because of the increased mobility. At the same time I started sessions in Homerton's woodwork shop, which led to even more mobility. I worked at getting the lines on a piece of wood perfect by slowly mastering the lathe. I had patience when I was doing something with my good right hand, but I was becoming increasingly frustrated that my left side was still refusing to show any real signs of improvement. My frustrations were eased by constant exercises. At no point during my stay at Homerton was I allowed to neglect my physiotherapy.

In March 1993 I did an exclusive interview with the *Daily Mirror* and they put my picture, the first of me since the fight, on the front page. It was a great picture which clearly showed my determination and at the same time just how far I had come since the fight. But inside there were several more pictures which showed just how far I still had to go. I looked like a brain-damaged man, and there was no escaping the truth they told.

Suddenly it felt like things were moving at a much faster pace, and by the end of March I was going back to Chingford for weekends. I had a big, comfortable chair which I would sit in and watch TV or eat Mum's food. I could even make breakfast for myself if I followed the instructions that were pinned on a kitchen cupboard. I still have the piece of paper which reads:

BREAKFAST
Do as much as you can IN STANDING

1 Collect milk and bread from the fridge, then put milk on the table.
2 Put bread in the toaster – check it is all switched on.
3 Collect cereal and jam from the cupboards – in standing.
   Take cereal, spoon and bowl to table.
4 Put jam on toast, then on plate, then take to table.
5 Put kettle on and collect cup, coffee and make it.
   Carer to carry coffee to table when completed.
6 Clear away items and kitchen/table surfaces afterwards

Now tick off on the chart about how well you have done!!

I was crawling my way back to health and a normal life – I was starting to see real progress.

In May 1993 a celebrity football match was organised for me at Highbury, and all the proceeds raised were promised to the Michael Watson Appeal Fund. It was a day that I looked forward to for weeks, and because it was really special it seemed to stay in my mind unlike many other things which faded in and out. I was dressed in a leather coat with a nice warm hat, and when I arrived at the ground I was given a shirt to wear. I changed into the shirt and was pushed out on to the pitch in my wheelchair by Kevin Campbell, my friend and Arsenal player, to the centre circle. I have no idea how many were there that day, but the chanting started and it seemed to last a long, long time. The love and support of the crowd touched me deeply. In my heart was the hope that I would return one day and walk on to it unaided. I told the friends that were with me that I would come back one day and do exactly that. I would walk all over that pitch and thank all the fans who had supported me in my career and all those who had turned out for the celebrity match.

The event was organised by Ambrose Mendy, and the Michael Watson Appeal Fund received a total of £86,000 pounds from it.

I found out shortly after the match that I was going to be released from hospital and that I would need that money to help convert my home in Chingford and make it more user-friendly for a man in a wheelchair. I would have to start planning the essential building work as soon as possible.

After twenty-one months in hospital and so many struggles I was finally going home for good and would have just a night and a daytime carer. I had two special friends and an old friend called Richard Humphrey, who I had actually sparred with twelve years earlier at Crown and Manor, who would take care of me. The three of them agreed to take over the next part of my rehabilitation. I knew that I would have to return to Homerton for the work to continue, and also attend a physiotherapy centre near Great Ormond Street Children's Hospital, and that I would have to make regular trips to see Peter. But essentially I was free.

Before I left for Chingford, Dr Richard Greenwood came to see me and admitted that he was amazed by my recovery. My injuries had been so serious that he considered my present condition to be 'nothing short of a miracle'. I thanked him from the bottom of my heart for all that he had done during my stay at Homerton.

I was a twenty-eight-year-old former professional boxer, and I couldn't walk, but to me the future looked bright.

How wrong I was.

When I got home, the gloom descended fast.

It was still like being in prison – the punishment continued. I had the words, but I couldn't get them out fast enough. I wanted to walk and run, but my body would not let me. I was becoming increasingly aware that I was trapped, and I was worried that I would never move on.

It was a grim period in my life and I needed all my faith to get through it. Peter asked me if I needed medication to help me try and lift myself from the gloom, but I told him that I had all the help I could get. I had my belief in God, though it was being put under immense pressure.

Peter explained to me that the depression was all part of the healing process – a simple case of post-operative depression, but I knew from conversations that I have since had with Peter that after brain surgery it can be very, very profound. It is an inevitable problem for survivors of traumatic head injuries, but with me there was an additional twist. I had been seconds away from realising a dream in the ring that night, just a few moments away from securing a future for my children and my family, when I lost it all. Later in my life, at a place called Headway, I met other head trauma victims who had also lost more than their memory and their independence when they were hurt.

I had thought that my lowest point was during the months at Homerton when recovery seemed to stand still and I felt I was actually going backwards, but when I went home, I had to deal with having lost everything. It was during this terrible time that I fully realised just how far I had fallen. I prayed for the strength to go on, to keep on fighting, and thankfully the carers I had with me at that time were as determined as me. I'm sure they felt low at times too, but they put all their energy into helping me to improve.

My carers had to be aware of my pain. If I had a headache and was dozing off, they would stop me and give me some more medication. If it was bad, and if they thought it was hurting me too much, we would go off to see Peter. There was a gadget called a shunt in my head that monitored the pressure on my brain. A tube ran from the shunt to the abdominal cavity, and it allowed any build-up of fluid to be drained from inside my skull. The shunt was adjusted and controlled by Peter, and he could take a reading of the pressure by holding another gadget close to my ear which was attached to a briefcase containing an array of dials and switches.

At the house in Chingford that summer I continued to sleep downstairs, and I had to use the commode when I needed the toilet. It was a long and boring summer, but by September 1993 I could stand in the living room with all three of my carers holding me. I could also, with a lot of help from the three carers and one or two other people, get up the stairs to my bedroom. I weighed nearly seventeen stone, so it is easy to imagine just how difficult and dangerous it was. Somebody once told me that I first made the enormous climb on 21 September 1993. It was certainly close to that dreadful anniversary when I pushed the door open on my bedroom once again.

I had a lift put in during early October of 1993. To me it was a great step forward, an almost miraculous advance, because suddenly I could get from room to room without the hands of my carers holding and helping me. It gave me control of my house. I was on my way to independence, and a life that nobody had predicted – but a life I was determined to have.

We put a ramp outside the back door for wheelchair access, which meant that I could go places. We started to go to the cinema, the shops, and of course for the obligatory sessions with the physios. I was still deeply concerned that I was not getting very much better and that I had reached the ceiling of my recovery. But I was determined – as determined as ever – that I would walk one day. I would defy the experts and walk from my bed to the bath and then walk downstairs. That seemed like a marathon to me back then, but one day I would do it.

In many ways the recovery from a head trauma is monotonous. It is the same thing, day after day after day. There was little change in the doom and gloom for me. Peter summed it up perfectly. 'Recovery is simply a fantastically boring existence.'

I was a full-grown man, but I had to ask for everything and have everything done for me. I needed help all the time, and I would often forget things just seconds after asking for them. It was not easy being me, and it was certainly not easy being one of my carers. I got impatient because I was frustrated. It was hard for my carers to know what to do. They were capable of looking after me physically, but it was much harder to help with my emotional and mental state. I would have mood swings. I would get very upset when people could not understand what I was saying because of my tongue being heavy in my mouth. It was frustrating for me and for my carers.

Looking after me has taken its toll on everybody over the years. Before the end of 1993 I had changed carers. My previous carers had both been true friends, and thankfully they still are to this very day. Richard remained and was joined by Alan and Christine, and my boring life on the endless road to an uncertain future continued.

I was getting closer and closer to taking a few steps, and I did take one or two, admittedly with three people holding me up, by about June 1994. The sessions in my living room in Chingford when my carers and friends tried to get me walking were always exhausting. One of my main problems was that I needed the exercise and the outside stimulation, but was always tired by it. My fighting stamina had withered, but my fighting spirit remained and was stronger than ever.

By the end of the summer of 1994, Richard and I were going to the local swimming pool for our own physio sessions. We would pay our admission price for an afternoon swim at the Track and Pool in Chingford and then get in with the regulars. I made a few friends, mostly men and women of seventy or more. We all seemed to be moving at the same pace. In the pool I could stand, and with Richard holding my hand I could walk. My every step was clapped and applauded by my elderly fan club and I was humbled to be part of their afternoon session.

One day I would walk from the changing rooms and dive into that pool. That was another promise I made to myself.

On 13 September 1994, my lawyer, Henri Brandman, issued a writ against the British Boxing Board of Control for negligence. If he had waited another nine days I would have lost the right to sue them. There exists a three-year limitation period in law, and we had only just beaten the deadline.

I was suing the Board for damages for personal injuries and loss as a result of the injuries sustained in my last fight. The Board, I argued, had neglected their duties to provide adequate medical care on the night.

I had fought for glory, honour and money in the ring. I had fought for my life in the operating theatre and now I had set in motion a third fight: the fight for justice.

Mum with Muhammad Ali when he came to visit me in hospital

With Peter Hamlyn, the neurosurgeon who saved my life

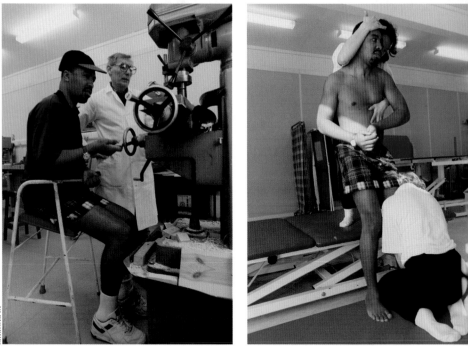

Doing various physiotherapy exercises to relearn movements
that had been lost, loosen my muscles and improve the
interaction between the left and right side of my body

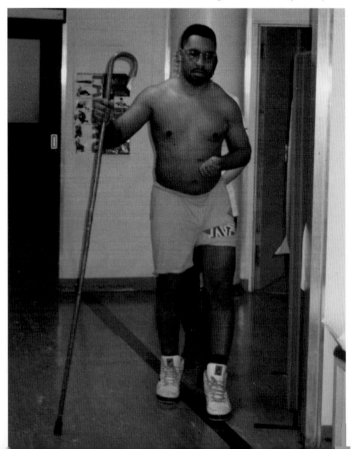

CLEVA

In 1993 a celebrity match was played at Arsenal football grounds
to raise money for my appeal fund

Arsenal player Kevin Campbell pushed me
on to the pitch in my wheelchair

GETTY IMAGES

Leaving court after the British Boxing Board of Control had been found guilty of breaching its duty of care

With my friend and carer Lennard Ballack, having a good time on holiday in Miami

Fronting a campaign
for the Disability
Rights Commission
in 2003

Receiving the
Helen Rollason
Award for courage
and achievement in
the face of adversity
from 'Marvelous'
Marvin Hagler

Attending the
Teenage Cancer
Trust concert

In Cornwall preparing for the marathon

With Lennard, just before the start of our long journey

Reaching the halfway mark
at Tower Bridge

Crossing the finishing line and
setting a new record – for the
slowest marathon in history!

Sharing the moment with Mum and Uncle Joe at the end

With Mum and Jeffrey after receiving my MBE

Taking time
to be with God

BRIAN MOODY

Taking time
to be just me

BRIAN MOODY

Chapter 10

I knew that issuing a writ and getting any form of justice were two very different things, but I had no idea that it would take quite so many years. The court case, when it eventually took place, and the years of preparation made the training period for a fight look easy. In the winter of 1994 I was ready, so I believed, for action, but in reality I was still several years short of fighting fit.

After an initial flurry of activity, the case against the British Boxing Board of Control continued slowly and formed a back-drop to my very ordinary life. I was still being looked at each week. During the sessions, physiotherapists would twist and manipulate my body and three years on I was still trying for my elusive first solo steps.

The constant memory tests with Richard were starting to help me, but all my progress was being measured against the expectations of the experts. If they were happy with a move-ment in my left leg, it didn't necessarily follow that I was pleased – I always wanted more from myself. I can still remem-ber the nights in Homerton when I struggled to make sense of my prison, but there was never any fear in my head. 'Get lost, you demon,' I would scream at it if ever it tried to get inside me and make me weak.

I was doing well but I wanted to do even better, to exceed some of the predictions. Nobody ever expected me to stand, but by 1995 I could stand with just one or two people holding me. My speech was improving all the time, but sadly my spirit would drop for the smallest of reasons and that caused me and the people that looked after me a lot of concern.

I was going out more and more and that undoubtedly helped me, especially if I was recognised. One of the highlights of my recovery around this time was a night in February 1995 when I was ringside at the London Arena for one of the most amazing fights that I had ever seen. My old adversary Nigel Benn was defending his World Boxing Council super-middleweight title against the brilliant and unbeaten American Gerald McClellan. I was in demand that night and posed for pictures and signed autographs. Although this was nice, it did remind me that my boxing life had been taken away, and my self-esteem did suffer.

There were shades of my rematch with Eubank in the build-up and, tragically, the similarity did not end there. After a truly savage brawl, McClellan was stopped in Round Ten. He was rushed to hospital and had a blood clot scraped from the surface of his brain. He survived and moved back to America. Subsequently, he lost his sight and most of his hearing. He remains in a bad way to this day.

When Benn left the ring that night, he paused by my wheelchair to kiss me on the head. He was also rushed to hospital in the second of the ambulances that were on standby but was, thankfully, only suffering from exhaustion and was allowed home that night. I enjoyed the fight, which I know is probably impossible for many people to understand.

In 1995 I went with Richard to Potter's House, a Pentecostal church in Walthamstow, to give a testimony. It was a very big occasion for me, because it was the first time I was due to speak in public. I was booked to speak on the Saturday afternoon during a weekend festival of gospel music. I spoke to about five hundred people for nearly ten minutes, and it was a tremendously uplifting experience. I was back in the public's eye after years in private, and it was the first of a thousand positive receptions from strangers that still never fail to make me feel humble. My only regret was that I spoke from a wheelchair. I told the brethren that I would be back without the wheels and that I would walk in to talk to them next time. The appreciation and applause that I received was incredible and I left the church that day feeling truly blessed.

This was just one more promise to add to the list I had started to compile in my head. The list was growing longer, but I was also getting better, and in 1996 I did indeed go back to Potter's House and, using Richard's shoulders as support, made a few hesitant steps from my wheelchair to the pulpit.

Peter and other experts had warned me all along that recovery from serious head injury can be slow, and that there was always the chance that it would stop abruptly. Each day I was aware that it could be the last day of my journey back to health, so each day in 1996 and 1997 I tried that bit harder to push myself just a little further. I knew that I was never going to wake up in the morning and suddenly be able to hop, skip and jump and have total recall. I was simply fighting for a future that was better than the previous few years.

In 1997 two important things happened. First, my old friend Lennard Ballack started helping Richard, and second, in September a lawyer called Michael Toohig took control of my case against the British Boxing Board of Control. These two men were to change my life for ever.

When Lennard appeared he made an immediate and huge difference to my daily life because he seemed to understand me far better than any of the other carers. Lennard always insists that by the time he came in to act as my carer, all of the hard work had been done, but that does not give him the credit he is due.

Before Lennard started working with me I went one day to his home and was waiting for him when he came in. He seemed shocked to see me standing and attempting to take a step. He always called my first steps 'massive limps'. We spoke that afternoon about him getting involved, and he agreed, but only if Richard would give him some training.

Lennard knew when and how to push me in the subtlest of ways, which was not that surprising to me because nearly ten years earlier he had taken Jeff under his wing and given him the confidence to work at the garage. He'd been gentle and sympathetic. Lennard has a natural instinct for knowing exactly when to push and when to back away. It is not just my opinion, because I have also spoken to Peter about Lennard's skills, and he agrees with me.

With Len helping Richard, and with the prospect of a new thrust in the case against the Board, which I knew would be good for me psychologically, I was feeling far more motivated than I had been for a long time. The Board had already put a measly offer on the table, but I wanted more because I felt I deserved more. I know that Henri Brandman would have been happy to continue with my case, and he was and remains a busy and popular solicitor and I still do business with him today.

The decision to switch solicitors from Brandman to Michael, who worked for Myers, Fletcher & Gordon, was made to give me a new angle on the case. A man called Al Hamilton, a journalist I had known for many, many years, had suggested the firm to Mum, and she had acted on his advice and set up a meeting. MFG was actually a Jamaican company with their main office in Kingston and a further two in New York and Hammersmith. It was decided at once to switch all of the papers regarding the case to Michael, and I thanked Al for his vision. Al stayed close to me throughout the years leading up to the court case.

There was, by the end of 1997, a problem with my legal aid, and the first thing that Toohig had to do was get that reinstated, which he managed. From that point on the only thing that mattered to me was the case. It took over my life completely, and Lennard was there to help at every turn.

In 1998 Richard left after five years of selfless devotion to my recovery. We had been through so much together. He had fulfilled his mission to see me rise from a bed and walk a few steps with the minimal amount of assistance. He had worked for such small sums of money and had worked such long hours that it was inevitable that he would have to leave at some point and think about his future. Before he walked away from the Chingford house, we spent an emotional afternoon back at the Crown and Manor club where we had first met about twelve years earlier. We climbed in the ring where we had once sparred and I was able to stand and move my body, using the ropes for support.

I went to stand in front of my favourite mirror, and with the slightest of steadying touches from Richard's fingertips I stood and threw a few rights. My left side was still not responding, but my right was working. In the mirror I could see the faces of my old trainers and other people I had known during my early fighting days at the club. It was my first appearance in a boxing gym, and people watched without speaking, but I could hear one or two grown men crying. I took a few of my 'massive limps' that day.

In early 1998 former world champion Colin McMillan organised an event to raise some money for the Michael Watson Appeal fund at a nightclub in Barking called Legends. I arrived by car with Len and Colin came to my door to open it and help me out. I took a few stumbling steps on my own, and then I noticed my old trainer, Jimmy Tibbs. He had seen me at four in the morning after the first operation and dozens of times since, but what he witnessed on that pavement was just too much for him and he broke down in tears.

I was still going to see Peter once each month and putting in as many sessions as I could in the gym, perhaps as many as three each week. I would use the standing frame to stretch my joints and do exercises for co-ordination and balance. I had been told by Michael that the court case, if indeed it did ever get to court, would require me to be in the best possible mental and physical condition.

Lennard and I started to spend a lot of time with Michael at his offices in Hammersmith, and he came out to Chingford when things started to really heat up. Mum and Uncle Joe were always present at the meetings and were still as important to my continued recovery as anybody. But I was starting to gain more and more independence – I wanted to be able to exist on my own and not dominate my mum's life quite so much.

At the time I was being taken four times each week to Uncle Joe's church, the Evering Pentecostal near Seven Sisters tube, and I was occasionally speaking from the pulpit. I would give thanks to God for giving me back my life. I had made a similar number of visits there each week when I had been younger, and there was something deeply comforting about being back in the place. It was a perfect retreat from the growing pressures of the case.

I provided Michael with a list of witnesses, and for the first time statements were taken that were then added to the evidence that he was compiling. Each visit to his law offices to go over details would leave me exhausted and exhilarated in equal measure. Michael was possessed by the case, and his enthusiasm was a sure sign that I had made a good choice.

I was more determined than ever to fight on, but so was the Board. I can remember that there was a feeling of growing anxiety when it became apparent that the Board were using a major law firm and had hired one of the top barristers. They had also employed a top neurosurgeon to counter Peter's claims. I'm told that when Michael spoke with Peter and mentioned the name of the Board's expert, there was a sharp intake of breath. I asked Peter about this much later and he told me that he had actually said: 'Oh shit.' The Board had serious intentions.

The respect for the opposition's legal team was something that never really bothered me, but when I found out that Peter considered their medical expert to be a brilliant mind, I started to understand just how big a thing this case was to other people. It was going to be a brutal and bruising confrontation, but I felt I had the right team behind me.

The hours and hours of preparation were never easy, but I see now that it was a kind of therapy, and with Len gently guiding me I was taking in and retaining far more information than at any point during my recovery so far.

On 13 October 1998 I had to make my statement. 'The Witness Statement of Michael Watson' is a harsh document because it puts my life of the last seven years into twenty-four paragraphs. It is a document without any glamour or glory. It

represents the facts and nothing but the facts about my condition, and it contains the chilling lines in point number 21, 'I am
not sure what my last memory was on the 21st September 1991
or when my next memory occurred. It was some years later.' The
day I made that statement was a very painful one for me.

The Board were constantly pushing for my legal aid to be
withdrawn, but I had no income and was totally dependent on
support, so we fought back and won every time. The money
from my last fight had disappeared a long time ago – any
suggestion that I was a rich man was absolutely ridiculous.
I needed the legal aid to keep the case going. The Board had
their big City firm with hundreds of lawyers, and I had Michael
Toohig and three others at MFG. The odds were tremendous,
but we were scaring them and making the running because we
refused to go away.

In early 1999 there was still a lot of work to do. We knew
that the Board thought we would never make it to court. Their
attitude upset me greatly, and when I was tired, and therefore at
my lowest, I would rant and rave against them. At times like
that, Lennard had ways to calm me and slow me down and
make me relax.

The meetings with Michael took an intense twist in 1999
because suddenly there were more and more legal representatives sitting in. The pressure was growing on me to perform and
perform well. Meetings were taking place in the chambers of my
barrister at Temple and there were days when I walked out of
there truly shattered. The discussions gave me an idea of just
how tricky my time in court would be. It made my little problem

against Mickey Duff/Morris Prager seem like a bit of harmless fun.

We had a date in June at the Royal Courts of Justice and in the weeks before everybody was getting very agitated. The Board made an offer to settle ten days or so before the hearing, but it was rejected. Their attempt at keeping me out of court increased to an amount of just £75,000 pounds with just days to go. Their effort barely stalled our last-minute preparations.

'It would hurt if the Board lost a case like this, and there is a chance that it may be settled beforehand,' claimed the Board's secretary John Morris, a prominent ringside guest on the night of my last fight.

On Monday 7 June 1999, there was one final meeting at Michael's office in Hammersmith. It ended in prayer with Mum, Uncle Joe, Michael, Len and Al all holding hands with me and asking for strength and guidance for the following day's case. We needed all the help we could get.

Tuesday 8 June 1999 was a beautiful day. The sun was shining down on me when the car stopped inside the special car park behind the Royal Courts of Justice in central London. Before Len could get out to open the door for me, it was pulled back by a man in a suit. He was not an usher or a security guard, just one of the hundreds of ordinary people that work inside the court complex.

'Welcome, Mike, we've been looking forward to this for a very long time,' he told me.

When I stepped out of the car I saw a bank of people. They

had come down from offices and other odd departments at the courts and were standing in the June sunshine waiting for me. I looked up and saw that people were looking out of windows, and then somebody started to clap and the noise just spread. I was getting a standing ovation on my first day in court.

I saw Michael standing there with a few members of our team and we all just waited for the people to stop applauding my arrival. It then took me a long time to get inside because they all wanted to talk to me and get an autograph. It was the most incredible reception in the oddest of places and by the time I went inside the court's dark halls I was feeling terrific. I was being wheeled because I didn't want to unnecessarily shock people with my attempt at walking. I was not looking for sympathy, just justice.

Mum, Uncle Joe, Al and a lot of my friends were there. Mum, as ever, had some of the sisters from the church with her, and in the dreary old court their colours looked splendid. I saw Sister Lynn and was reminded of all the nights she had sat in lonely vigil by my bed in the intensive care unit at Bart's. It was all flooding back to me, and I said hello to some other people that I had not seen since the night of the fight.

We were due in the Lord Chancellor's court at 10.30 that morning and had arrived nice and early. I wanted us to find a room and pray, and I knew that Michael was ready and waiting for any late and dramatic developments from the Board's legal outfit. It was a high-adrenalin time and I was buzzing. Len was forced to dab my right brow and get rid of the sweat the whole time. The leg and arm on my left side barely worked and nor did

the sweat glands. I only sweat on my right side – there is a clear
and visible line down the middle of my body.

At just a few minutes before ten, just as most of my family
and friends were going to a small room to pray, there was a lot
of rushed movement over by the court's door. I saw Michael in
conversation with a few other men and then I saw others run
over and join the talk. There were no raised voices so I realised
it was not a row, and I had never seen most of the men before,
so I realised it was not my legal team having a final conference.
I told the people at the door of our makeshift prayer room to
wait a second, turned to Len and motioned for him to wheel me
away from the door and closer to Michael.

A minute or so later Michael came over to me. He coughed
and suggested that we go somewhere private. Uncle Joe, Mum
and Al had joined us.

'Michael, they've made an offer. It's the best so far. They've
offered £180,000,' he told me.

There were fewer than thirty minutes to go before we were
due to take our seats in court. They had waited to make what
they thought was an offer I could not refuse.

We talked for a few minutes and Michael went back to their
legal team with our demand. We asked for £220,000.

A few minutes later he came back.

'They refuse to move higher than £180,000,' he told me.

We were all in a tiny room. He looked at me. It was very quiet
and still, with just the distant murmur somewhere of people
going about their business. The £220,000 would help me set up
a lifestyle. I had a decision to make.

I sat and thought about the years of struggle before I made any money in the ring, the years of pain after my last fight and the years in front of me. The Board had gone from £75,000 to £180,000. They had refused to go up an extra £40,000 and save everybody the hell of a long and vicious court hearing. This was not enough for what had been taken away from me.

I turned to Michael Toohig in that tiny room and told him to go back and tell them, 'Michael Watson says no.'

Michael went to tell them, and minutes later we took up our positions in court as if nothing had happened. The room was packed on that first day, and one of the first things on the schedule was a screening of the fight against Eubank at White Hart Lane. I had watched it so many times that I was familiar with every second of every round, but this was the first time the fight had been shown in public since ITV went off air that night.

In 1991 22,000 had sat and shouted from the temporary seats on the pitch at Tottenham's ground and over twelve million people had watched it on TV – their broadcast had ended with me still in the ring. In court that day there were fewer than forty people. It was a terrible fight for some of my friends and family to watch, and Mum cried as I came to rest on the canvas after the stoppage in Round Twelve. Her sobbing was the only noise in court because the segments of the tape that showed me collapsing and being carried out had no sound. They were silent and horrific images.

When the film had finished, and after lunch had been eaten in the same tiny room in which I had turned down the Board's latest offer, I was required to give evidence. I had to go through the ordeal of the witness box because the Board wanted to ask me questions. I was ready for it. I knew they would try and catch me out by somehow finding a weakness in my memory. I knew they would fail because I had spent so many hours preparing, starting right back when Henri Brandman was in charge and would give Richard Humphries hundreds of pages for me to read. I knew the case inside out and was looking forward to getting in the chair.

The noise in the room when my name was read out was the strangest noise I have ever heard. I never thought that shock had a sound, but that morning I heard it loud and clear. I was needed in the witness chair to give evidence about the night that I was left injured and I would be giving evidence in front of the men that I was charging with being responsible for my injuries. Few people would have believed that I would ever have the chance to stand up and tell the story. But some of the believers were in the court to support me, and I could feel their love.

I was in my wheelchair, but I decided that at thirty-four years of age I was going to walk to that witness chair on my own. I was not bothered if it took me two minutes or two hours. I was determined to do it.

Uncle Joe wheeled me to the front of the court and stopped to the right of the judge. He then helped me up, but that was all he did before moving back slowly with the chair. I was on my own in the court, and in front of me, about twenty-five feet away to the left, was the chair and the few steps that led up to it.

I set off for that chair with the same desire that I once had in the ring. I was facing John Beckles again at York Hall on my nineteenth birthday. I was inside the supertent on Finsbury Park looking across at Nigel Benn in 1989. I was waiting for Chris Eubank in the chill of a late September night in 1991. I had the same indomitable spirit that Peter Hamlyn had witnessed on the first night he went inside my skull in search of a blood clot that was minutes from killing me. Annie Meharg had felt that spirit on the day in 1992 when I had screamed out her name to end the agony. Len had seen it a thousand times when I went just one step further than I had the day before.

There were various people from my past life in the court that day. I saw their faces out of the corner of my eye as I started the long walk. I could feel the pressure of their eyes on me, but I knew a few sets were turned away. I was a man who was taking steps that nobody ever believed he would.

I paused when I reached the chair, and a court official moved forward to offer me a hand up the few steps. I smiled and refused because I had to do this on my own. I pulled myself up. Later that night Tim Westwood, the DJ who had created my ringwalk music for the Eubank rematch, said I looked like a mountain climber near the very peak of a climb that has taken him all his life to complete. That was how I felt when my bum finally came to rest in that seat.

There was a pause in the court for me to have a sip of water and mop my right brow. Then I had to start talking.

I told them that I thought I could remember being in control of the fight and that I was thinking about becoming the world champion. I added that I believed there was a fantastic future in front of me. The court heard my witness statement clearly, and the fact that I was able to back it up sent a message to everybody in that court that I was not joking. I was serious. I had prepared my body and mind for a long fight.

Mr Colin Mackay, QC, representing me, argued that if I had received the proper medical treatment in the ring I would never have sustained the brain damage that I had suffered. He showed that the Board introduced several safety measures after my fight and that had these been in place, most specifically the availability of resuscitation equipment, I would not be in the condition I was in.

'There is no earthly reason why such facilities should not have been in place on the night of the fight. If that rule had been in force, Mr Watson would not be as he is today,' Mr Mackay said.

The Board argued that even if the equipment and measures that they later introduced had been available, I would still have suffered the same level of brain damage. Mr Mackay fired back at their every assertion during the case, and there were evenings when it was obvious that he had given everything.

I never lost control in the box on the day that I was made to speak. It was exactly what I had prepared for, and each day until the hearing ended I returned to court and listened and waited for the end result. We had a debriefing every day, and Mr Mackay made a special effort to go through the day's events with me.

The hearing was expected to last six days, but in the end it went from 8 June to 22 June, and then Mr Justice Ian Kennedy retired to find a judgement. He was being asked to decide only the issue of liability. If I won, a hearing for damages would then be arranged.

We expected him to get back to us by the end of June, but he kept us waiting for three months before calling a judgement date for Friday 24 September 1999.

The Honourable Mr Ian Kennedy found that there was a duty of care, and that the British Boxing Board of Control were in breach of that duty. It meant that it was more likely than not that had their new regulations been in place, I would have made a full recovery and suffered no disability.

I had won a major victory and I was heading for the Law Reports once again. The Board's QC applied for an appeal, but the judge refused. They later applied to the Court of Appeal and were granted the right to appeal. I had won but there was no money, and after they were granted the right to appeal, there would not be any until their appeal was heard.

The frustrating years were not over.

My dad died in December 1999. In 1991 he had been flown over by a tabloid paper when I was in Bart's and had arrived unannounced at the doors to the intensive care unit. He stopped outside the door to the ICU and waited until one of the nurses noticed him. She asked if she could help him and he told her that he was there to see his son. Mum spoke very briefly to him. He only stayed a few days before flying back to Jamaica.

MICHAEL WATSON'S STORY

My life continued as usual after the hearing. I stayed in contact with Michael and we waited daily for news of the Board's appeal. I had been warned that it could take a year for it to be heard, and that seemed totally unfair to me. There were reports that I was looking for three million pounds, but they were grossly exaggerated and I spoke to some journalists to let them know that their figures were wrong. It looked like there was an attempt to paint me as a greedy money-grabber intent on crippling the Board. That was not true. I had been willing to walk away on the day of the hearing for £220,000. I was not being greedy, I just wanted to secure a reasonable lifestyle. I was not talking about a beach existence somewhere exotic, I was talking about being able to pay carers for the rest of my life, because that was my reality.

I had started to attend a unique club called Headway shortly after the hearing, and I found the place to be both uplifting and exhausting. The original building was near Homerton hospital, but they have since moved to a better site near the old boxing venue of Shoreditch town hall.

Headway is for people of all ages who have suffered a brain injury. It offers the unusual type of support that people who have suffered traumatic head injuries need. We feel isolated and lonely, and the extreme emotions we experience are influenced by what we have lost. Our problems are not just medical – we have a variety of problems, but they are not recognised – people don't understand what has really happened to us. Everybody at Headway was leading a normal life before something happened. Some had suffered an aneurysm, but

168

others had far more colourful histories. One guy there was beaten by prison officers, another was a victim of the IRA terrorist attack on Canary Wharf, and several were survivors from car wrecks.

There is nowhere quite like Headway because of its mix – there are times when it is impossible to work out who is working there and who is part of the club. It is run by Miriam Lantsbury and Tony Bonfil, and I'm supposed to be part of the Tuesday club, but now I miss far more sessions than I attend. In 1999 and 2000 I was a regular, and it helped me control my moods because I was mixing with people who understood me. They were the same as me. If I thought my loss that night in the ring to Eubank was severe, there was always somebody at Headway who had lost more.

At Headway I started to make sense of the dreadful stories that Peter Hamlyn had been telling me about for several years – about families that had split apart when one member had suffered a brain injury. There were wives and husbands who simply could not cope with losing the person they had fallen in love with and married. The person who comes out of hospital is never the same, and many marriages collapse, and with the breakdown the lives of the many children involved suffer. The person with the injury often ends up at home with their mother, but too many end up in homes. Until I went to Headway I had no appreciation of just how serious a crisis exists in the care of brain injury survivors.

At Headway I have met people whose families have turned their backs on them, and I have met people with mums just like mine. There are also people who have received large compensation payments, but left homeless, without a family and with very few friends, they are no happier than others.

Visits to Headway drain me because the other members ask a lot of me. The constant questioning can be exhausting. I try and give them as much of me as I can. I like to think that I inspire the people there in the same way that I have been inspired by the people that I have met there over the years. When I leave there these days, I stagger out and say, 'Thank you, Jesus, I have reached a lot of people today.'

In May 2000 I was ready to go back and thank the fans at Highbury for their generosity in 1993 at the fundraising match on my behalf. On that occasion I was stuck in a wheelchair, but when I returned with Lennard and Michael as company for a match against West Ham United, I was walking on my own. There were 38,000 people in the beautiful old stadium, and when I walked out on to the pitch everybody started to sing, 'There is only one Michael Watson.' It was a memorable day, which gave me a great feeling.

We found out that the Board's appeal would be heard at the Court of Appeal in October 2000. We were all due in court in front of the three Lord Justices of Appeal, and on 17 and 18 October we listened to a lot of the old arguments. Lord Justice Philips, the Master of the Rolls, Lord Justice Laws and Lord Justice May sat and deliberated. A judgement day was set for 19 December 2000.

None of the team could contemplate defeat after so many years. We were confident of winning and confident that this would be the end of the affair. Surely they would just admit defeat and let me get on with living my life.

The three Lords upheld the original decision and I won again.

The Board immediately applied for leave to appeal, and for the second time they were refused, but when their legal team applied to the House of Lords, they were given permission. By this time it was already 2001, and we were told that we would have to wait at least another eighteen months.

I have broken down many, many times since I came out of the coma, but the night of the Board's successful application to the House of Lords was different. I was not crying tears of pity or pain, I was crying tears of utter frustration at my situation. After the first Eubank fight at Earl's Court in 1991 I had sat in my changing room and asked the question: 'What do I have to do to win?' When I found out that I would have to wait another eighteen months to find out what my settlement would be, I felt exactly the same way. I had no answer in 1991 and I had no answer ten years later in 2001.

By the time the Board had gone into administration and it looked like I would never get a penny. Things looked worse and worse. I needed all my faith to get through those dark, dark days.

Then, out of nowhere, Frank Warren emerged. I had known him for many, many years though he had never promoted me. As he put it, 'I've never made a bean out of Michael Watson.'

Warren charged on to the scene and turned it all upside down. He told the Board to be at the Grosvenor House Hotel on a certain date, and told Michael Toohig to be at the same place for a without prejudice meeting. He spoke with Al Hamilton and guaranteed my presence and that of Mum and Uncle Joe at the meeting. Warren got us all together in a room in April and went to work brokering a deal and putting an end to the crazy situation.

'Right, we've got to get this situation sorted because this is a disgrace,' Warren said.

He believed that silly amounts of cash were trickling away from me and into the pockets of law firms. He reminded everybody that he knew a thing or two about costs, having been at the centre of dozens of cases. He never blamed either side, but he was clearly upset with the Board's inability to budge on certain issues. The meeting was often very, very hostile, but Warren made it clear from the start that it would only come to an end if a proposal for a resolution was agreed.

'This is not about the law, it's about that man over there in the wheelchair, and it's now time to do the right thing,' Warren shouted at one point.

He told the Board to settle it or he would not pay any more licence fees of any description. Since he was the Board's highest contributor, that was a very serious threat to make. I could tell he was not joking – it was clear that he was utterly serious.

'This has probably cost over a million pounds in legal fees, and it has to stop because it is damaging to the sport,' Warren continued.

It was getting late before the Board agreed to sell their

building, which was in a prime site near London Bridge. It was the first time they had mentioned selling, but not the first time it had been mentioned to them. I left after six hours. Michael stayed a lot later to try and get me a result.

A framework was agreed, and after many meetings a deal was reached. We then had to go back to court to see Mr Justice Buckley at the Queen's Bench Division and tell him that the Board were dropping their appeal. He praised me for my courage.

At the time the agreement was reached it was nearing 21 September. This year was especially significant because it was the tenth anniversary. A film crew from the BBC made a documentary about me. It was called *Fighting Back: The Michael Watson Story*. It ended with Eubank and me reunited in a hotel room – a scene that required great courage of us both. It felt good. I had forgiven Chris a long time ago. I knew that it had not been intentional, and it could so easily have been the other way round.

The film raised my profile, but my bank balance was still in a terrible state and I needed some of the money that I was due. The settlement deal is complicated, but I will eventually receive something in the region of £400,000. Warren proposed that he would put on a charity night in aid of my Appeal Fund, and took the precaution of covering his own back by insisting that the Board write to every one of their licence holders to ask them if they wanted to make a contribution. Just one man, a trainer in London, wrote back and sent in a cheque for £1,000.

There was only one place that could possibly hold my testimonial evening, and that was the Grosvenor House Hotel. I had been in and out of the revolving doors dozens of times since the first conference to publicise the first Eubank fight in May of 1991, and on Monday 8 July 2002 over twelve hundred people packed the Grand Ballroom in my honour. It was once again an evening that humbled me. I was honoured to have there Lennox Lewis, Eubank and hundreds of other fighters from my life, and from the years before and after my fighting era. Even Jake LaMotta flew in from New York.

I gave thanks that night at the Grosvenor House and bowed my head slightly during the fights that took place. I closed my eyes and thought about my life up until that point. I was overwhelmed. I knew that it was surely a miracle that I was sitting there at that top table. I thanked God once again for saving my life and my soul that night at White Hart Lane. I knew that I had become what I was because of what happened to me then. I had been saved by God, and he had given me a destiny to help and be an inspiration to others.

When I next stood up I was lighter, and people looked on with open mouths as I climbed into the ring with Lennox and Eubank.

'Something happened to you tonight, bro,' Lennard told me when it was all over.

At the Grosvenor that night nearly £180,000 was raised from the auction and ticket sales for my Appeal Fund. I was given the cheque a few weeks later by the Prime Minister Tony Blair, and that was wonderful.

In just over a year my life had changed drastically. I had

recovered from the despair I experienced when I found out that the Board had been granted leave to appeal the previous April, and at the Grosvenor I had been filled with the rapture and joy of pure celebration. I was as happy as I could ever hope to be.

After the testimonial at the Grosvenor I had a talk with Peter, who was also the founder of the British Brain and Spine Foundation. We talked about a lot of different things, and the Flora London Marathon was mentioned.

A month or so later I was at the Whitechapel Hospital in London's East End for my annual medical check-up, and the idea of completing a marathon was mentioned again. Both Lennard and I laughed at the suggestion when Peter started to talk about it. He came across as if he was joking at first, but as he continued talking, I realised he was serious.

'Are you serious?' I asked him.

'I'm very serious,' he replied.

I asked a few questions and he gave me a few details. I liked the idea that I would be raising money for the British Brain and Spine Foundation, and I liked the idea that if I finished the race, it would be against the odds. I liked that idea very much. I have always enjoyed challenges.

I stood up and got ready to leave.

'Have a think about it,' Peter said.

I turned to him immediately.

'I have,' I said. 'I will do it.'

It had started as a joke, or so I thought, but in the space of thirty minutes it had developed into a new and difficult challenge for me to overcome. I had just said yes to taking part in a marathon when I still needed help walking from the car to a meeting.

However, it was exactly what I needed to continue making progress with my endless recovery. It tickled my taste buds, and I love the taste of victory. I was hungry for a new test, another personal challenge, and the London marathon was perfect. If I could complete the distance, I would not only have overcome an enormous physical barrier but also raised money for a charity that had given me a great deal.

In the car I turned to Lennard. He was smiling.

'What?' I asked him.

'A marathon is a long way. That's a long way for you to go,' he told me.

'What do you mean me? You're coming too,' I told him.

'I knew you were going to say that,' he replied.

All I had to do was add about twenty-six miles to the 385 yards I could walk at that time. It was going to be an epic struggle, and one that would require every ounce of strength, determination and faith.

Chapter 11

In November 2002 I met up with Peter Hamlyn, who by now had become a friend, and we spoke again about the Flora London Marathon. It was, he assured me, a very long way from the start to the finish, and he was not certain that I would be able to actually complete the distance.

I told him that faith is a powerful weapon, and that the hardest bit of the marathon would be the victory salute at the end, but I knew it would be the most difficult of all the trials and tribulations I had overcome since September 1991. Although it seemed impossible, I felt fully confident that I would complete this marathon.

I listened as Peter told me that most marathon runners hit the wall after about twenty miles, but that I would hit a wall after a hundred metres and would keep on doing that until the end or until I was forced to withdraw. I knew he was not trying to put me off – all he wanted to do was make me aware of just how serious the marathon challenge would be for me.

He was smiling and shaking his head as we sat in his office near Marylebone High Street in central London. He could tell from my short answers that I was serious about walking the twenty-six-mile course and finishing it. He knew more about my determination and desire than anybody else did. He had seen me fight when I was unconscious, and watched me carry on fighting when I was barely conscious. He knew all about my indomitable spirit.

We agreed that I would take part in the marathon in aid of the Brain and Spine Foundation, as discussed before, and it was also arranged that I would captain the *Daily Telegraph*'s marathon team. There was no way out of it once I had given Peter my word, and by the end of November news of my latest and possibly greatest sporting event was announced.

I was deeply honoured to be involved with the *Daily Telegraph* team and their continued and generous association with the Brain and Spine Foundation. At one of the press conferences, which took place at Highbury stadium, I told everybody that as far as I was concerned the race was accomplished. I was back on the top table and I wanted to make an impression, and I promised that I would set a milestone in the marathon for all others to follow. The moment the cameras were back on me I started to get a familiar buzz, and I soon realised that the challenge was giving me inspiration. It felt like an echo of the weeks before my first world championship fight with Chris Eubank when I had held a press conference in the same Highbury room to help promote the fight.

I knew I was up against the odds, but that was nothing new to me. I looked at the twenty-six miles and I looked at my condition, and then I looked at other problems that I had overcome in my life. I thought about the night I fought against Nigel Benn at Finsbury Park in 1989, and every single day of my recovery since the last fight with Eubank. I remembered learning how to tie my shoelaces, brush my teeth and make a cup of tea. I understood that twenty-six miles was a long, long way but I knew something not many people understood, which was how far a person travels from a coma to being able to hang out the washing in the summer sun. I had been on an impossibly long journey for many, many years.

'Let's go for it!'

I meant exactly what I said, and from that point in December I started to prepare for something that I really had no right to be taking part in. I could not walk more than a few hundred metres at a time, and even then I was very dependent on Len's shoulder for a bit of extra support and balance. I had four months to get ready – the start date was 13 April – and I had a body that I needed to train to rise to an unbelievable challenge.

There had been a time when I had had legs and a body that I could no longer use, but that had changed. I now had a mind with full understanding, and I knew that I could get my body fit and ready for the marathon. My efforts would help others by raising money and showing them that there was always hope, even in their darkest moments. It was important to me that others would benefit and take inspiration from what I was about to put my body and soul through. I had been saved for a purpose, and now I had found the challenge that would fulfil it.

To be a true champion you have to go down and come back up again, and I had been on my way back for a long, long time. I had stopped taking life for granted when I emerged from the darkness of my injury, and I now saw life as a great gift and something to be celebrated each and every day.

The marathon would add to my successes, and with my faith I could do it. I knew I could move mountains. The marathon would give me a platform to spread the word and show people how powerful faith and belief can be.

In the days over Christmas of 2002 I had a lot of time to think about the miles that lay before me. I had a picture of the Flora London Marathon in my head, and I could see skinny African champions, people collapsing, crowds packing the capital's streets, women in wheelchairs and the thousands and thousands of fun runners. I was not sure where I fitted into the plan, except that I knew I was not a fun runner, because I had been through hell and the run would probably take me back there briefly.

In early January 2003 I had to go for a series of medical examinations to make sure that my physical condition matched my ambition and desire. The tests took place at the Sports Medicine Department of the Mile End Hospital, and I was put through a series of gruelling tasks. The experts took notes and asked me questions, but I was not feeling great and I was struggling a bit with my walking as I went up and down the room. I ended up on a couch with a few pillows propping my legs up. I have days like that, and I knew I would have to use all my mental power to make sure that I was fighting fit for the marathon. I was in the race to go the distance – I'm not the sort of person to start something and not finish it. I'm a perfectionist.

After watching me and measuring my steps, the marathon's medical director, Dr Dan Tunstall, and Dr David Perry, a rheumatologist and noted sports physician, declared that I could take part and that I had a chance of finishing. The marathon's director, David Bedford, was stunned by my iron will, but he was not convinced I would complete the distance. I left the hospital that day exhausted but more determined than ever to reach the finish line, however many days it took me.

Len had spotted some roads suitable for training, and we started with short walks in the cold January air in Edmonton, Stoke Newington and Turnpike Lane. We settled for the streets because we knew the course would provide a lot of natural hazards and we wanted to be prepared. One day I stumbled and fell, and other days I was too tired to continue after twenty minutes. It was a struggle, but we began to increase the distance each day and I could feel a difference. I was walking for longer – but I was tired and I ached.

Patrick Draydon, a fitness trainer joined Lennard from the start to help with my training. Pat worked out a routine for us to follow, and he was also keen to work on my balance. He introduced gym work and put me through some explosive sessions on the exercise bike that were at a totally different tempo from the pace I set on the street. He wanted me to be able to vary my speed if I had to, and he wanted me to know that I could do even more if I had to.

The marathon training helped me regain the feeling that I had last had in the Black Lion pub in Plaistow, East London, during my weeks of training for the Eubank rematch. It all came back to me, how I used to train for a fight, and it inspired me to push harder and harder.

In Stoke Newington we would eat at the Blue Legume each day before taking off down Church Street and turning right at the lights on to the High Road and then to Stoke Newington Road and eventually all the way to Kingsland High Street. I knew all the streets, and hundreds of people each day would call out my name from shops or cars. I was building a following and my routine was attracting a lot of regular well-wishers.

Life on the streets was a motivation, even if there were hazards in the shape of pavements and cars and bags of rubbish. I was getting in some serious walks and I could feel that same old buzz that I had experienced all those years earlier, but my body had changed and I needed an extra something.

One day on the streets of Stoke Newington I found what my body was looking for. On the High Street there is a Chinese medicine shop, and as I turned the corner I stopped and just went inside. I have no idea what made me go in. I had walked past the door dozens of times.

Inside I was met by a woman called Lilly. She asked if she could help me.

'I don't know why I'm here. I just had to walk in,' I tried to explain to her.

Lennard was at my side and Lilly looked at him, but he didn't have an answer. At that moment Dr Ming Lu came out of the back room and introduced himself to me. He explained what he did and how it could help me prepare for the marathon. I was sent to his shop by a greater power, I know that now. It was as if I was called there.

Dr Lu explained to me about the benefits of acupuncture and other Chinese methods of healing. He was a calm and intelligent man. I agreed to return for acupuncture and had my first session with him in February. I went twice each week until the very start of the marathon. I had sixty-minute sessions with him and forty minutes was spent having traditional acupuncture down my paralysed left side. I would spend the last twenty minutes having a full body massage, and I found my energy levels rose considerably and I was far less tired.

After acupuncture I could walk normally. There was no limp and I felt on top of the world. I could actually kick out my right leg like a footballer. When I left the treatment room I always felt like running the marathon, not walking the marathon, and my pace would increase on those afternoons.

In March I went to Hustyns, a private resort in Cornwall, for three weeks of intensive training. The fresh air and the walks on nearby beaches and across the tops of cliffs only added to the stamina and condition that I had acquired on the streets of north-east London. However, I was still a very long way short of being ready to complete a marathon.

At Hustyns Ron Grinstead, a former Olympic wrestler, put me through my paces. In addition to the beautiful local natural attractions they have a track for their guests. The track is one mile long, and at first I could complete it only with the help of his shoulder. It sloped in places and was a pleasure to walk, but the fact remained that with less than a month to go I was still unable to complete a mile on my own.

After three days I did my first mile without any assistance, and from that moment Ron, and my personal coach, Patrick, set me harder and harder targets. It was exactly like being back in the gym with Jimmy and Dean shouting and telling me what to do and how many rounds were left.

Hustyns had a boxing ring and I took advantage of it to put in a few rounds of shadow-boxing. It was amazing being back in the ring, moving and throwing out my right, and taking my time to go back to the ropes. On one particular day Gary Newbon, the ITV reporter that interviewed Eubank in the ring after our last fight, arrived with a film crew. I could tell from his look of utter amazement that nobody had told him just how fit and ready I was. He filmed me in the ring at first, and then as I effortlessly hit a speedball with fast rights. He was just the latest in a long line of people I had left speechless in the years since my last fight.

The training regime at Hustyns was tough and there were nights when I was too exhausted to talk. I had felt like that during the darkest days of recovery when my body had been put through hours and hours of intensive physiotherapy by the experts that helped rebuild me, but back then I had been stuck in the prison of my disabilities, whereas at Hustyns I was able to walk fast, punch a bag again and push myself. It was both a shattering and a fantastic experience.

Ron and Patrick kept pushing, and in those three weeks I went from walking one mile in one hour to completing two laps in just ninety minutes. I was getting closer and closer to readiness – and the start was getting closer and closer too. I had found a strength and calmness at Hustyns, and I knew during the last few days at the luxurious retreat that I would finish the marathon in style. The early walks, the late afternoon sessions in the gym and tiredness were worth it. I was fitter than I had been in over eleven years. I was ready for the London marathon.

I returned to Chingford for a few final walks and some time to get my head in perfect shape. A week before the marathon, just as I was getting a bit agitated, I had a visit that lifted my spirits. Arsenal's physiotherapist, Gary Lewin, arrived at my house in Chingford with the FA Cup. I was staggered when he came into the living room holding the gleaming silver trophy, but Lewin was more interested in the World Boxing Council belt that Nigel Benn had given me, which was hanging over my sofa.

Having the FA Cup in my hands was a great lift and it set me up for the start line in Greenwich Park the following Sunday morning. I wanted the race to start. I was ready and I was getting the right nerves, just like a boxer does before a big fight.

I was awake at 4.30 in the morning and looking out of my window over the streets of London, and I was full of adrenalin. I recognised the feeling. It was a feeling from my former life as a championship boxer, and it stopped me from sleeping. I had not had it for a very, very long time and I knew that the start gun would not come a minute too soon.

At 7.30 I met the team in the lobby at the hotel and was immediately surrounded by people wishing me luck and asking for autographs. It was the start of a truly remarkable week of attention that took me by surprise. We drove to Greenwich in South London, and there was a tremendous buzz, an excited feeling in the air. The closer we got to Greenwich Park the bigger the crowd was.

We had access to the elite athletes' warm-up area and met up with Peter there. Len and I were given our official numbers with our bibs. I was 60199 and Len was 60198. I was raring to go and it was not yet 9 a.m. Already it was obvious just how special the day would be.

I recognised the calm feeling from my days in the ring, and being surrounded by other top athletes, all of whom had that look of focus that only the best have. I had had that look each time I walked from the dressing room to the ring. No fear, just 100 per cent confidence in my own abilities and a faith that nobody will ever be able to shake. I felt just the same that morning, ready for another big fight.

Bedford, the race director, found time to come over and wish me luck. I told him what I tell everybody, which is that it is not luck, it is faith and belief. He went away happy, but I wondered if his concerns about me finishing were causing him problems. Maybe if I failed he would be held responsible. He knew it was not a publicity stunt and that everybody else who had played a part in getting me ready could testify just how hard I had trained. The week in front of me would be the hardest of my life.

I heard Peter talking to a few journalists, but I didn't look over. I just listened as he told them once again about my miracle of a recovery.

'Michael has no business to be walking to the end of the road, never mind starting a marathon. If he achieves it, and it is a big "if", it will be one of the greatest physical achievements the marathon has ever seen,' Peter told them.

At that moment I was sitting back relaxing in a folding chair and drinking a cup of tea.

Outside the elite athletes' tent, the first group of collectors with their buckets from the Brain and Spine Foundation were waiting for me. The rest of the *Daily Telegraph*'s sixty marathon runners had already left – they were also raising money for the BSF. By the time we set off that morning there were probably over seventy collectors, and their spirits never once dropped throughout the whole walk. They were an inspiration to me because on each new street or road they would make as much noise as before and fill the pavements with their buckets held out. During the next seven days a few celebrities joined in the act, and they were even more persuasive.

The theme for the marathon was 'Give It Up for Michael Watson', and very early on in the walk I realised just how many people still knew who I was. From the very first steps on the streets of South London the shouts of encouragement and the noise of coins dropping in the buckets were all I could hear.

The elite athletes had left fifty minutes before I took my first stumbling step, but the streets were still full – word seemed to have spread that I was coming by.

The first day of that enormous week was often overwhelming for me and for my team. People cried, people shouted my name, and they just kept coming out on to the streets to see the fighter that had come back from the dead.

The adrenalin was still pumping and I completed the first mile in just twenty-two minutes. When I passed the marker, a band beside the road started to play 'You'll Never Walk Alone'. It was very, very moving, and I only kept going by taking long, deep breaths.

At The Mitre pub in Woolwich I stopped and went in to thank the landlord, Wayne, who had collected £160 from his lunchtime punters. The atmosphere in the pub was electric and I left them singing my name when I continued on my way.

The marathon's cleaning lorries had passed me by about the three-mile mark and Paula Radcliffe had finished her marathon, but the crowds were still out cheering my every step. I found out later that Paula had set a new world record and broken her old one by two minutes. I was not in the race to set a world record, but I was doing something that few people had ever dreamed achievable.

I stopped on the first day to help a wheelchair athlete from Japan who had broken down, because I found all the wheelchair athletes particularly inspirational. Stopping was not part of the plan because I needed momentum from staying at a regular pace, which is why when people came out of pubs and flats to give me money I could not stop and chat. Len or Peter would gently tell them to walk with me if they wanted to say a few words. I had to keep going, but wanted people to know how much I appreciated what they were doing.

During the first day, some of the people who came out and gave me money or encouragement truly lifted my spirits. Old people literally emptied their purses and wallets into buckets, and some women sneaked a kiss before dropping in a note.

I completed five miles that first day before coming to a stop at the junction of Woolwich Road and Hardman Street. I was greatly relieved to climb on board the double-decker bus that I was using for breaks and for eating during the marathon's course. I was hurting, but I was also ecstatic from the reception I had received during every long step of the way. I had twenty-one miles to go and my body was already aching in places that had never ached before but I knew I would continue. I knew I would finish what I had started. I had known I would from the moment I had given Peter my word seven months earlier.

A meal had been arranged at the Thistle Hotel for the evening of the first night, but once I got back to my room and saw the bed I realised how utterly exhausted I was. I knew I had to eat, but it took all of Len's best lines of encouragement to get me to go back downstairs. It was Sunday night and the plan was that I would walk down the Mall near Buckingham Palace at about noon on the following Saturday. As I collapsed into bed that first night I could not imagine what condition I would be in by then. I knew I would be totally worn out. I could feel the blisters coming already, and I knew they would not just vanish. But the spirit of the people had played a major role in getting me through the first day. I couldn't wait to get back out there and get close once again to the people cheering my every step and filling the buckets.

On day two my team did a marvellous job to get me out on the street and fired up for another day. I'm not normally very good in the morning, but for the marathon I had to change the way I think. I had to get up early and have a positive frame of mind or we would fall behind, and if I dropped a single mile, the entire marathon would be at risk.

We had all started to walk by 8.30 and this time there were no helicopters and no big crowds behind the barriers. In fact there were no barriers – just me in the road with Len, Patrick and Peter and the small army of collectors with their buckets. It was business as normal on the Woolwich Road that morning, and that meant a lot of smelly traffic and big lorries, but we pushed forward and the people came.

Frank Maloney joined me for most of the day. Maloney made an immediate impact because, armed with a bucket, he actually moved out into the middle of the traffic and stopped cars.

We met a policeman, but because he was in uniform he couldn't give us any money. However, at the end of the day there was a knock on the door of the bus. It was the policeman, this time in civilian clothes, and he added to our collection.

There was one particular incident on day two that has stuck in my mind – so many of the things that happened during the marathon are just a blur. I remember seeing this guy walking towards us with a really fierce-looking dog. It was a bull mastiff, I think, and the guy had come out of some flats and into the road and was walking towards us. He was looking at us intently.

He stopped and put his hand in his pocket and pulled out a few hundred pounds in large notes, and as I walked past him he clutched my hand and gave them to me. He never said a word, just handed over the money and carried on walking.

I gave the money to one of the women with a bucket and then Lennard caught up with me. He had been behind me at the time and had watched the man stop. He had then watched him stop just a few feet after giving me the money and noticed that there was a pained expression on his face, so he had stopped to see if he needed help.

'No, I don't need any help now, mate, thanks,' he said to Len, and then he told him that in 1991 he had been a ticket tout and was working the streets near White Hart Lane when I met Eubank. He was young then and cash was easy to come by, and he had acquired a gambling habit. On the night of the fight he had had several big bets that I would lose. He won a lot of money.

'I've just given Mike everything I owe him,' he told Len.

Maloney was not the only special guest to walk with me on the second day – I was also joined by Alex Robinson, a twelve-year-old boy who was walking for the first time since being run over by a car in May 2002. It felt great walking with Alex. Before joining me on the marathon, he couldn't walk. He had watched me and wanted to get up out of his chair and join me.

I had inspired him – which was part of the reason for walking the marathon. I wanted to reach people like him who had given up hope of ever achieving their dreams. I had been told I would never walk or talk, and I had proved everybody wrong. I wanted other people to feel inspired to achieve the same thing.

Alex walked with us for two miles before his Achilles tendons started to hurt, and then he had to stop. His bravery reminded me of all the days and nights when I had managed to push the barrier and go just a few paces more.

At the end of day two I had walked nine miles in total and my feet were in a mess. I had blisters on my toes, and the aches and pains from the previous evening were now far worse. We had to throw away my bloody socks when I stopped walking and buy some replacements. The drive back to the Thistle in the bus from the point in Surrey Quays where we had called a halt was a luxury, because I was no longer on my sore feet. When we arrived I needed to rest a hand on Lennard's shoulder to make it to my room. I was exhausted and exhilarated at the same time.

We left south London on Tuesday and crossed Tower Bridge, which was a great feeling because it was the halfway mark. Thankfully, my painful feet and aching bones had responded well to treatment and there was an extra little skip in my step. The crowds that were coming out to greet me appeared to arrive at exactly the right time – we seemed to be a great excuse for entire offices and other work places to empty.

The sound of coins being thrown into buckets was all that

mattered to me because my aim was to finish the marathon in one piece and raise as much money as possible for the BSF. The BSF's fundraising manager, Veronica Martin, told me that some people had called our credit card line, donated by the *Daily Telegraph*, and pledged as much as £2000.

Veronica was impressed, but I wanted more and more money and I used the diary column that I was writing for the *Daily Telegraph* that week to ask readers and spectators to come out and support me. Gareth A. Davies, the reporter who was helping me with the diary, was with my team the whole time and helped to keep me motivated on a lot of occasions.

Another fighter who had suffered a horrific injury in the ring joined me on day three. His name was Robert Darko, and he had collapsed shortly after losing an amateur fight in the London championships at York Hall in 1990. Peter had operated on him, and it was tremendous to have him on the walk with me. There are a lot of boxers out there who have suffered injuries in the ring, and most are anonymous.

At the end of the third day I was getting on top of the marathon schedule, and that night I surprised everyone in my team by being full of life. Nobody could have guessed that I would feel so fit halfway through a marathon that the experts doubted I could complete. I was looking forward to the finish line and putting an end to the pain all over my body, but at the same time I was loving every second of the public's attention. I was reaching out and touching people and raising the profile of the charity.

Wednesday and Thursday were draining days, but the crowds still appeared at every step and friends continued to come out and walk with me. I had completed seventeen miles by the end of Wednesday, and from that point on I could smell the finish.

Early on Thursday, Britain's first Olympic boxing gold medallist for thirty-two years, Audley Harrison, came out to support me and add his unique fundraising methods to the Michael Watson show. Audley went one better than Frank Maloney by actually stopping traffic. All of the traffic! He simply marched across the lanes and put up his hands until the cars stopped and then, like a mad general in battle, sent all of the collectors to wave their buckets at the windows of the stationary cars. Frank Warren also joined me on the Thursday.

That day I walked through Canary Wharf and was overwhelmed by the noise and the reception I received in the glass valley of buildings. As I approached I could see that thousands had come out from the offices to pack the streets, and for about an hour all I could hear was their thunderous applause. It quite literally knocked me over. I look back at that day and think of it as the day I brought London's business world to a standstill for a short time.

At the end of day five I had completed twenty-one miles. I was on fire and most of the heat was in my left foot where a blister from day two had become infected. It was a horrible and painful cut, and when I took my shoe off that night we all knew that there was a serious problem. The blood had leaked through my sock and stained my training shoe.

Patrick took charge and went out and bought some Epsom salts to bathe and cleanse the wound. It was a long night and everybody held their breath in the morning when the foot was inspected. I was given the green light to continue, but I had made up my mind to go forward even if the doctor had said no. I was not going to fail because of a cut on my toe.

On Friday the sun was shining. There was a terrific feeling at breakfast after my toe was passed fit to walk, and a great atmosphere from the moment we started walking. It remained that way all day long with our solitary and devoted little party.

Ashley Cole, the Arsenal and England defender, pulled up next to me on the road and handed over a £50 note. Jim McDonnell, a former quality fighter and one of the best trainers in the country, joined me. Jim had finished the marathon in the top four hundred the previous Sunday and promised to come and walk with me. Jim and I go back a long way and I always enjoy being in his company.

I walked by the Tower of London and posed for pictures with Beefeaters and tourists and other well-wishers. During my walk in front of the Tower I had one of my many unplanned calls of nature. It was generally easy to stop in a pub and have a pee, but in front of the Tower I sensed there could be a problem.

We had attracted a few hundred walkers and they were in a good-natured group behind Lennard, Patrick, Peter and me. It often happened that people just tagged along for a while. The procedure when I needed to use the toilet was to send

Geraldine, my agent, out on a scouting mission. As I negotiated the cobbles by the River Thames in front of the magnificent Tower, she hurried over and pointed at some portaloos on the other side of a grassy area right by the river bank. I was getting increasingly desperate at this stage, so I simply took off – but the entire group that had been following me walked with me! When I came out I received a standing ovation from the hundreds who had waited patiently for me to finish my private business.

This was typical of that Friday, a day when the car horns honked almost all of the time – and when comedian Ricky Gervais joined our team the party atmosphere really took off. But one problem with all the fun was that it was easy for me to get distracted, and I did actually fall when my foot hit the kerb during Friday's walk. Luckily, Lennard was there to rush forward as I tumbled and he managed to get his hands under my head and shoulders to stop me from crashing into the pavement. We stood up and gave thanks, because only Lennard would have known to react so fast. Other people would have just thought I was walking awkwardly and then it would have been too late to grab me.

Even though we were all having a lot of fun on Friday, it was a punishing day. I marched on like a holy warrior when the pain came and ignored the cut on my toe, my sore ankle and my muscle strains. Each step was hurting me and I had to focus on the end of the day when I knew I would have only 1.2 miles left to complete.

My support team had started to relax a little and so I decided to tease them a bit by making out that I couldn't go any further after we stopped for lunch. We all went to the bus and I told Len, Peter and Patrick that I was finished.

'The pain is too much, I've got to call it off,' I told them They stared back with open mouths.

'It's been a good attempt, and nobody will ever accuse us of not trying. I can't walk another inch,' I continued.

Still none of them spoke. I could see tears in all their eyes, so I thought I'd better stop tricking them, but then I thought, 'No, make them suffer a bit more.'

'My legs are killing me, my knees ache, my back is sore. I've had enough. I quit,' I added.

Then Len smiled. One word I'd used warned him it was all a con. He laughed out loud and Patrick and Peter looked at him as if he was losing his mind.

'He's winding us up. He would never "quit", he doesn't know how to *quit*,' said Len and then I laughed. He was right.

At the end of day six I was within touching distance of my destination and it was a wonderful feeling. We returned to the hotel and had a nice quiet evening in our own company, though there was certainly an air of celebration.

Late on the Friday night I spoke to Wayne Malcolm, the pastor from the Christian Life Church in Walthamstow that I had been attending each Sunday for about six months. Pastor Malcolm told me that I had been an inspiration to his flock during my visits and that everybody attached to the church was praying for me.

The following morning I would be joined by some special

people for the last mile of the 2003 Flora London Marathon. I knew the organisers planned to re-erect the finish line gantry for me to walk under. Dipping my head below the clock was something that I had been thinking about an awful lot.

On the Saturday morning I spoke to Lennard at about six o'clock.

'Are you ready, bro?' he asked.

I was ready, I had been ready for a long time.

We went to a café in Aldwych to have breakfast with Chris Eubank. It was a very emotional meeting and he seemed in awe of what I had achieved, not just in the last six days but in the twelve years since his fists had come so close to ending my life. Eubank was going to join me later, and we said goodbye and set off for the last leg of my big walk, my latest fight against the odds.

I was in no hurry to end the epic journey – there wasn't that far to go – and I took my time. I wanted to do it all again, to go back through the streets and see and meet all the people one more time and thank them all again. It had been a truly memorable journey and it would be impossible to list all of the people who had touched me – the thousands who came forward and gave money to the BSF's army of bucket carriers.

As I walked the final section in front of crowds that were swelling with each and every step I took, I started to think through the people who had made the marathon so very special, and the people who had made the impossible possible. It was a long list which stretched back to the doctor and nurse who took me in at the North Middlesex hospital at midnight that Saturday night in 1991, and who saved my life for the first time, and which stretched across the years and included hundreds of devoted people – they all went through my head. It included the bag woman at Bart's, the bucket carriers who had never stopped, my team, whose endless belief was so moving, and the Flora organisers who had been professional and sensible at all times.

However, it was the people of London and the people who came to London to watch my journey who got to me most deeply during my week on the streets. I had seen grown men and women crying as I walked past them, and I had smiled or raised my right fist to show them my respect for them. But what can you say to a man like the homeless guy under the bridge on the Embankment, who left his cardboard box and came over in his old clothes to give me the 70p that he had collected that day?

The list of heroic acts by the public was long indeed, and it made me feel incredibly humble to know that they had all come out because of me.

Time stood still on that Saturday morning. I could see so many faces and I seemed to know a lot of them. There were people I recognised from my days in boxing and people I knew from my years in recovery. It seemed that everybody who had ever met me was on the streets of central London that morning for my final mile. I saw women from the Blue Legume café in Stoke Newington, the base for many of my early training walks. I also saw fighters I knew from Colvestone and Crown and Manor, and members from Headway.

I was joined by Eubank and a very special friend of mine, Spencer Oliver, for the final walk to the line. Oliver lost his European title and, like me, fell into a coma, but he is alive and well today because of the safety regulations that were introduced after my last fight in the ring. 'Michael Watson nearly died to save my life,' he told a radio journalist who walked next to us for a few minutes.

With the finish line in sight I put an extra bounce in my step even though I was tired and my feet hurt. I was so excited and the adrenalin was pumping through my body. I was loving every single second of it and I wanted it to never stop. Len, Patrick and Peter had moved away to give me extra space, but we should have gone across the line together because we had been a great team.

My mum was waiting on the far side of the line smiling and looking very proud. She had my medal and was ready to put it over my head and round my neck when I finally crossed.

The 2003 London Flora Marathon was nearly over. I had just a few paces left before I finished what many people were calling one of the most amazing sporting achievements in recent years. Others simply called it a miracle. I knew that it was possible only because of the strength that came through my faith in Jesus Christ.

I walked across the barrier and split the tape. The clock above my head stopped. It read 6 days, 2 hours, 27 minutes, 17 seconds. I, like Paula Radcliffe, had set a record – for the slowest marathon walk in history.

I was in Mum's arms and I could hear her telling me that she loved me. I could feel people patting me on the back. Peter was talking to a reporter, reminding her of what I had overcome and just achieved.

'Just six months ago he struggled to cross a room on his own. This is quite incredible,' I heard him say.

Peter's gentle words of coaxing all those months ago had benefited the Brain and Spine Foundation by just over £200,000. The devoted men and women with the buckets who had accompanied me from the start to the end had collected £25,000, the phone lines had generated another £50,000, and £25,000 was received in cheques that arrived at the BSF's offices. The *Daily Telegraph*'s team of runners had generated another £100,000.

I had completed the Flora London Marathon against the odds. I had finished the latest and possibly the greatest challenge of my life, and I thanked God for the strength he gave me to get through it. I felt whole. It was as if I had come full circle. And it felt good.

I needed a few days to recover, and then I returned to the endless list of engagements and award ceremonies that I attend. I try and lift the spirits of everybody that I come into contact with, and if I can help raise the profile of a good cause I will always help.

In addition to the ongoing work for the Brain and Spine Foundation, I have become increasingly involved with the Teenage Cancer Trust. It is work that I value because I have seen the immediate effects of their fundraising efforts. The Trust raises money to help place cancer units for children inside

National Health hospitals. I have been touched so deeply by what I have seen that I just have to continue doing what I can to help.

After the marathon, the awards and recognition for my achievement were truly amazing. In December 2003 I was invited to the BBC's *Sports Review of the Year*. It was a magnificent event and I was stunned when 'Marvelous' Marvin Hagler appeared on the set and presented me with the Helen Rollason award for courage and achievement in the face of adversity. Nigel Benn and Chris Eubank joined me, and for the first time ever we were gathered together in the same room. It was a wonderful end to a memorable year.

The new year got off to a great start when I was awarded an MBE for services to disabled sport. Going to the Palace with my mum and brother Jeffrey to receive the medal from the Queen was one of the proudest moments of my life. It was a great honour to be acknowledged in this way. My life has served many purposes and I will continue to take it in new directions.

I am proud to be the people's champion. I was put, and kept, on this earth for a reason – to be an inspiration to others. And I give thanks to God for every day of my life.

MICHAEL WATSON

Former Commonwealth Middleweight Champion
Former WBA World Middleweight Title Challenger
Former WBO World Middleweight Title Challenger
Former WBO World Super-Middleweight Title Challenger

Islington, London, England   Middleweight   D.O.B. 15.03.65

Career Record

1984

Oct. 16	Winston Wray, Royal Albert Hall, Kensington, London	WTKO	4

1985

Jan. 26	Johnny Elliott, York Hall, Bethnal Green, London	WTKO	8
Apr. 14	Denis Sheehan, York Hall, Bethnal Green, London	WTKO	3
Jun. 5	Gary Tomlinson, York Hall, Bethnal Green, London	WTKO	4
Nov. 5	Mark McEwan, Wembley Arena, Wembley	WTKO	6

1986

Feb. 12	Karl Barwise, Royal Albert Hall, Kensington, London	WTKO	3
May 7	Calton Warren, Royal Albert Hall, Kensington, London	WPTS	6
May 20	James Cook, Wembley Arena, Wembley	LPTS	8
Nov. 4	Alan Baptiste, Wembley Arena, Wembley	WPTS	8

1987

Jan. 19	Ian Chantler, Grosvenor House Hotel, Mayfair, London	WRTD	4
Feb. 22	Ralph Smiley, Wembley Conference Centre, Wembley	WPTS	8
Mar. 19	Cliff Gilpin, York Hall, Bethnal Green, London	WPTS	8
Oct. 5	Frank Morro, Café Royal, Piccadilly, London	WTKO	4
Oct. 28	Sam Houston, Wembley Arena, Wembley	WTKO	2

1988

| Feb. 3 | Don Lee, Wembley Grand Hall, Wembley | WTKO | 5 |
| Mar. 9 | Kenny Styles, Wembley Grand Hall, Wembley | WTKO | 9 |

Apr. 13	Joe McKnight, York Hall, Bethnal Green, London	WTKO	4
May 4	Ricky Stackhouse, Wembley Grand Hall	WTKO	4
Jul. 28	Israel Cole, Las Vegas, USA	DPTS	10
Oct. 24	Reggie Miller, Blazes Club, Windsor	WTKO	5

1989

Jan. 18	Jamie Shavers, Royal Albert Hall, Kensington, London	WTKO	3
Mar. 8	Frankie Owens, Royal Albert Hall, Kensington, London	WRTD	3
May 21	Nigel Benn, Finsbury Park, London	WKO	6
	Challenge for the Commonwealth Middleweight Championship		

1990

Apr. 14	Mike McCallum, Royal Albert Hall, Kensington, London	LKO	11
	Challenge for the WBA Middleweight Championship of the World		
Nov. 18	Errol Christie, N.E.C. Birmingham	WKO	3

1991

Jan. 23	Craig Trotter, International Hall, Brentwood	WRTD	6
	Defence of the Commonwealth Middleweight Championship		
May 1	Anthony Brown, York Hall, Bethnal Green, London	WKO	1
Jun. 22	Chris Eubank, Earls Court, London	LPTS	12
	Challenge for the WBO Middleweight Championship of the World		
Sep. 21	Chris Eubank, White Hart Lane, Tottenham, London	LTKO	12
	Challenge for the WBO Super-Middleweight Championship of the World		

Fights: 29   Won: 24   Lost: 4   Drawn: 1   KO's: 17

Index

acupuncture, 183
Alexandra Palace, 66, 70
Ali, Muhammad, 17, 95, 119;
  Rumble in the Jungle, 57–8
Amateur Boxing Association
  championships, 22, 24, 32–3
America, 65, 73, 153
Andries, Dennis, 21, 23; warns
  Michael, 31–2
Arsenal football club, 85
Arum, Bob, 76
Atlantic City, 71
Ayling, Andy, 83

Ballack, Lennard, 15, 51, 59; helps
  Watson, 154–7, 159–62, 165,
  170, 174; enters London
  marathon, 175–6; marathon
  preparation and support, 179,
  181, 183, 186, 189–92, 195–8,
  200
Baptiste, Alan, 44
Barker, Russell, 34–5

Barking, 156
Barkley, Iran, 73
Barwise, Karl, 41
BBC, 37; *Fighting Back: The
  Michael Watson Story*, 173;
  Sports Review of the Year, 202
Beckles, John, 25–30, 31, 32, 37,
  40, 165
Bedford, David, 181, 186
Benn, Nigel, 48–9, 65, 66, 74, 76,
  77; Watson fight, 50–9, 60, 79,
  81, 83, 165, 179; wins and
  retains middleweight title, 71,
  73; Eubank fight, 78; supports
  Watson, 100; McClellan, fight,
  152–3; gives Watson WBC belt,
  185; joins Watson and Eubank
  on BBC, 202
Bethnal Green, 16
Blair, Tony, 174
Bloomsbury Crest hotel, 19
Bonfil, Tony, 169
Boxing Monthly, 65, 126–7

Brady, Terry, 52, 53
brain injury survivors, 168–70
Brandman, Henri, 74, 78, 79, 80, 82, 115; and case against Board of Control, 150, 164; Watson leaves, 155, 158
Brentwood Leisure Centre, 79
bribery, 64
British Boxing Board of Control, 38, 55, 75, 90; contract, 72, 80–1; safety proposals, 131–2; sued by Watson, 150, 151, 154–5, 158–67; granted leave to appeal, 167–8, 170–1, 175; appeal to House of Lords, 171; in administration, 171; settles with Watson, 172–3
British Brain and Spine Foundation, 175, 187, 193, 198, 201
broadcasting, 37, 64
Brown, Anthony, 81–2
Bruno, Frank, 119
Buckley, Mr Justice, 173

Caesar's palace, 47
Café Royal, 85
Campbell, Kevin, 85, 145
Canary Wharf, 169, 194
Canning Town, 84
Cappuccino, Frank, 87
Carney, Mick, 20
Chantler, Ian, 44
Chingford, 94–6, 117, 140–1, 143, 145–7, 149, 156–7, 185
Christian Life Church, 197
Christie, Errol, 78–9
Christine (carer), 149
Cole, Ashley, 195
Cole, Israel, 47, 50
Collins, Simon, 44
Collins, Steve, 68, 77
Colvestone gym, 14, 20–4, 31, 38, 92, 199

Connor, Roy, 20
Cook, James, 42–3
Coyle, John, 57, 58
Crown and Manor club, 17, 19–20, 21, 46, 145, 156, 199

Daily Mirror, 90, 91, 141, 142
Daily Telegraph, 131, 132, 193; marathon team, 178, 187, 201
Dalston, 14
Darke, Ian, 109
Darko, Robert, 114, 193
Davies, Gareth A., 193
Davies, Ronnie, 100, 101
Dawn (dietician), 95
Dawson, Jill, 136
Delaney, Gary, 95
Detroit, 24
DeWitt, Doug, 71
Douglas, Rod, 114
Draper, Ernie, 86
Draydon, Patrick, 181, 184–5, 190, 195, 197, 200
Duff, Mickey: manages Watson, 37–8, 39, 42, 45, 46–7, 62–5, 68, 130; Benn fight and doubts, 48, 51, 52–7, 59; love of boxing, 65; argues with Michael, 69–70; end of relationship with Watson, 71–4, 77; legal proceedings, 74, 75, 78, 79–81, 160
Duran, Roberto, 17, 24, 53, 70
Dyer, Darren, 22, 28

Earl's Court, 83, 86, 171
Edmonton, 181
Elliot, Johnny, 40
Enfield, 1, 3, 5, 14
Eubank, Chris, 65–6, 79, 114; Benn fight, 78; first Watson fight, 81–2, 83–9, 91, 92, 99, 171, 174, 178–9, 191; rematch, 92–5, 97–107, 120, 152, 165, 169,

179, 182, 184; visits Watson in hospital, 121; fight on video, 134, 163; attends Watson charity night, 174; breakfast with Watson, 198; joins Watson in marathon, 200; joins Watson and Benn on BBC, 202
Evering church, 40, 96, 111, 116, 157, 161

Finsbury Park, 51, 53, 56, 59, 60, 65, 69, 73, 165, 179
Fitzroy Lodge club, 20
Foreman, George, 57–8
Francis, Roy, 103, 106, 114
Frazier, Joe, 138–9

Geraldine (agent), 196
Gervais, Ricky, 196
Gilpin, Cliff, 45
Gloucester, 32
Graham, Herol, 62, 64, 66
Greenwich Park, 185–6
Greenwood, Dr Richard, 133, 146
Grinstead, Ron, 183–5
Griver, Harry, 23, 26–9, 32–6, 38–9, 43
Grosvenor House Hotel, 24, 83, 94, 95, 97, 119, 171, 174–5

Hackney, 132
Hagler, Marvin, 70, 202
Hall, Graeme, 24, 32
Hamilton, Al, 149, 160–2, 172
Hamlyn, Dr Peter, 155, 165, 193; arrival at Bart's, 112–14; medical care for Watson, 116–18, 120–3, 125–6, 134, 137, 145, 147, 157; prepares Watson's mother for his death, 121; *Daily Telegraph* report, 130–2; recommends safety measures in boxing, 131–2; and

Ali's visit, 138; predicts depression and boredom, 146, 148; warns of slow recovery, 153–4; on legal case, 158; stories of brain injury survivors, 169; friendship with Watson, 177; and London marathon, 177–8, 186–7, 189–90, 195, 197, 200–1; founder of Brain and Spine Foundation, 178
Hammersmith, 155, 157, 160
Harrison, Audley, 194
Hart, Colin, 77
Hassidic Jews, 1
Headway Centre, 147, 168–70, 199
Hearn, Barry, 63–5, 68–9, 75, 78; Watson joins, 79; and Eubank fights, 81–2, 90, 91, 92
Hearns, Tommy, 53, 70
Hemsworth, Ross, 73–8
Highbury, 85, 144, 170, 178–9
Holyfield, Evander, 127
Homerton Hospital, 128–9, 130, 132, 134, 137, 139, 140–3, 145, 147, 152
Hope, Maurice, 38
hospitals, 6–7; *see also* Homerton Hospital; Mile End Hospital; North Middlesex hospital; St Bartholomew's hospital; Whitechapel Hospital
Humphrey, Richard, 145, 149–50, 151, 154–6, 164
Hustyns, 183–5

International Boxing Federation, 69
Islington, 10, 26, 51
Islington club, 26
ITV, 71, 87, 104, 184

Jamaica, 1, 2, 45, 168
Jim (dietician), 95
John Paul II, Pope, 141

Junior Amateur Boxing Association
    finals, 19, 20

Kamel, 86, 95, 96, 97, 108
Kaylor, Mark, 84–5
Kennedy, Mr Justice Ian, 167
Kilbride, Cherry, 136–7
King, Don, 76
Kipps, Bob, 19, 20

Laing, Kirkland, 21, 23–4, 127
LaMotta, Jake, 174
Lantsbury, Miriam, 169
Las Vegas, 47, 50
Laws, Lord Justice, 170
Lawson, Harry, 25, 26
Lee, Dangerous Don, 47
Leonard, Sugar Ray, 53, 70
Lewin, Gary, 185
Lewis, Lennox, 174
Lilly, 182–3
London Arena, 152
London Bridge, 173
London marathon, 175–6,
    177–201
Los Angeles, 24, 33
Lu, Dr Ming, 183
Lynne, Sister, 124, 161

McCallum, Mike, 60, 62, 77;
    Watson fight, 64–71, 72, 82, 84,
    85, 88; phones Watson after first
    Eubank fight, 89; advice to
    Watson, 99
McClellan, Gerald, 152–3
McDonnell, Jimmy, 101, 195
McEwan, Martin, 40
McGuigan, Barry, 101
Mackay, Colin, QC, 166
McKenzie, Duke, 127
McMillan, Colin, 156
Magri, Charlie, 38
Malcolm, Wayne, 197

Maloney, Frank, 190, 191, 194
Manchester (Jamaica), 45
Martin, Veronica, 193
May, Lord Justice, 170
Meggi, Leroy, 138–9
Meharg, Annie, 135–6, 165
Mendy, Ambrose, 53–5, 60, 73–5,
    119, 145
Michael Watson Appeal Fund, 141,
    144–5, 156, 173
Mile End Hospital, 180
Milton Keynes, 20
Mitre pub, Woolwich, 188
Montserrat, 12, 13
Morris, John, 160, 165
Myers, Fletcher and Gordon, 155,
    159

National Amateur Boxing Club
    championships, 24
National Association of Boys' Clubs
    semi-finals, 20
NEC, Birmingham, 78
Nevada rules, 47
Newborn, Gary, 184
North Middlesex hospital, 109–11,
    131, 199
nubbins, 41–2
Nunn, Michael, 68, 77

Odeon, Leicester Square, 85–6
Oliver, Spencer, 200
Olympic games, 22, 24, 25, 30,
    32–3, 34, 36
Owens, Franklin, 48, 51

Paris, Sister, 5, 10
Perry, Dr David, 181
Philips, Lord Justice, 170
Plaistow, 93, 182
Potter's House, 153
Powell, Dean, 93, 95–7, 106–7,
    184

press, response to Michael's injury, 111–12, 116, 20
Preston, 32–6
purse bids, 63–4
Pyatt, Chris, 95

Radcliffe, Paula, 188, 200
Rawling, John, 109
Rectory Road, Stoke Newington, 2, 6, 133; fire, 7–11, 13–14
restraint of trade, 74, 80–1
ringside resuscitation, 132, 166
Robinson, Alex, 191–2
Robinson, Jon, 93, 95, 116, 119
Robinson, Mark, 116
Rocastle, David 'Rocky', 85
Romeo, 18, 19
Rosenthal, Jim, 59
Royal Albert Hall, 31, 39, 41, 48, 51, 69
Royal Courts of Justice, 80–1, 160–1

Sanderson, Garry, 19
Schumacher, Brian, 33
Scott, Mr Justice, 80
Seccombe, Eric: Watson's trainer, 24–9, 32–6, 38–9, 41, 43, 48, 60, 109; acquires professional trainer's licence, 36; preparation for Benn fight, 51–4, 57, 59; preparation for McCallum fight, 66–8; press conference, 74, 76–7; preparation for Eubank fight, 84, 86–9; end of relationship with Watson, 92–3
Shapiro, Stephan, 109
Sheehan, Dennis, 40
Smiley, Ralph, 44
St Bartholomew's hospital, 111–12, 124, 130, 133, 137, 141, 167; bag lady, 112–13, 120, 199
Stamford Hill, 1, 3

Stephenson, George, 112
Stoke Newington, 181–2, 199; *also* Rectory Road
Stracey, John H., 38
Sun, 77, 90
Surrey Quays, 192

Teenage Cancer Trust, 201
Thorne, Lenny, 31
Tibbs, Jimmy, 84, 86, 88–9, 184; takes over as Watson's main trainer, 92–3; and Eubank rematch, 94–8, 100, 102, 104–7, 108; religion, 95, 98, 115–16; attends Ali function, 119; sees Watson take steps, 157
Tomlinson, Gary, 40
Toohig, Michael, 154–5, 157–63, 168, 170, 172–3
Tottenham, 1, 2, 85
Tottenham town hall, 26
Tower Bridge, 192
Tower of London, 195–6
Trotter, Craig, 79
Tunstall, Dr Dan, 181
Turnpike Lane, 181
Tyson, Mike, 126–7

Walthamstow, 153, 197
Warren, Carlton, 41–2
Warren, Frank, 63, 171–2, 173, 194
Watson, Dawn, 3
Watson, Derek, 45
Watson, Jamilla Mary, 44, 46, 60, 68, 70, 104; response to father's injury, 142
Watson, Jeffrey: accident, 3–5, 115, 132, 133, 136; Rectory Road fire, 7–11; special school 14; going to church, 15–16; involvement in Michael's career, 19, 36, 51; garage job, 154–5

Watson, Jimmy, 1, 3, 5, 14–15, 36; lack of interest in Michael's career, 19, 46; returns to Jamaica, 45–6; visits Michael in hospital, 46, 167–8; death, 167–8

Watson, Joan: arrives and settles in England, 1–3; Jeff's accident, 3–5; extra sense for her children, 6; cooking, 7, 38, 95–6; Rectory Road fire, 7–11; faith, 11; church, 15–16, 46; involvement in Michael's career, 19, 36–8, 40, 51–2, 66, 71–2, 80, 89–90, 96; husband leaves, 46, 168; and Michael's injury, 109, 111, 114–17, 119–24, 126, 128, 133–4, 136, 142; accompanies Ali on visit, 138; involvement in case against Boxing Board of Control, 157, 160–3, 172; greets Michael at end of marathon, 201

Watson, Layla Ezra, 47, 60, 68, 104; response to father's injury, 142

Watson, Michael: childhood, 2–16; Rectory Road fire, 7–11, 13–14; schools, 14–16, 133, 141; going to church, 15–16, 46; takes up boxing, 17–20; joins Colvestone gym, 20–4; jobs, 21, 44; Beckles fight, 25–30, 31, 32; warned by Andries, 31–2; loses Preston fight, 32–6; turns professional, 35–9; joins Mickey Duff, 37–8; diet, 38; first professional wins, 39–42; overconfidence, 42–3; need for friends, 43; fatherhood, 44–5, 46, 47, 61; religious faith, 45, 62, 71, 73, 80, 95, 98, 126, 129, 130, 141, 146, 160 170, 174, 176, 177, 180, 186, 200–2;

fights Americans, 46–8; technical draw with Cole, 47–8, 50; split with Zara, 48, 52, 61–2, 66, 79; Benn fight, 50–9, 60, 79, 81, 83, 165, 179; loneliness, 52; money, 61, 63, 71–2, 74; plan to start removal company 61; McCallum fight, 64–71, 72, 82, 84, 85, 88; change of image, 66; broken nose, 67–8; ring rust, 68, 69, 82; argues with Duff, 69–70; end of relationship with Duff, 71–4; proceedings against Duff, 74, 75, 79–81, 160; press conference, 74–7; self-management, 75, 90; misinformation, 77; Christie fight, 78–9; People's Champion, 79, 85, 96, 202; joins Barry Hearn, 79; first Eubank fight, 81–2, 83–9, 91, 92, 99, 171, 174, 178–9, 191; brings in Jimmy Tibbs as trainer, 84, 92–3; weight, 85–6, 93; press conference, 90–1; rematch with Eubank, 92–5, 97–107, 120, 152, 165, 169, 179, 182, 184; end of relationship with Eric Seccombe, 92–3; carried from ring, 108–9; taken to North Middlesex hospital, 109–11, 131; transferred to St Bartholomew's, 111–12; critically ill, 112–24; Zara visits, 119–20; Eubank visits, 121; signs of recovery, 124–9; love of boxing, 126; transferred to Homerton hospital, 128–9, 130; determination, 133, 143, 148, 176; paralysed left side, 134, 156, 161, 183; watches video of fight, 134–5; Ali visits, 138; rehabilitation, 132–40; home for

Christmas, 140–3; access to children, 142; slow recovery, 143–50; home for good, 145; post-operative depression, 146; sues Boxing Board of Control, 150, 151, 154–5, 157–67; able to stand, 152; attends Benn–McClellan, fight, 152–3; speaks at Potter's House, 153; first steps, 154, 156; legal aid, 155, 159; speaks at Evering church, 157; 'Witness Statement', 158–9, 166; Eubank fight screened in court, 163; Board of Control appeal, 167–8, 170–1; time at Headway, 168–70; reception at Highbury, 170; case settled, 171–3; elated by charity night, 173–5; agrees to enter London marathon, 175–6, 177–81; marathon preparations, 181–5; effects of acupuncture, 183; training at Hustyns, 183–5; Gary Lewin brings FA Cup, 185; walks marathon, 185–201; breakfast with Eubank, 298; Eubank joins in marathon, 200; involvement with Teenage Cancer Trust, 201–2; awarded Helen Rollastone trophy for courage, 202
Watt, Jim, 37
Webb, Ray, 67–8

Wembley, 22, 34, 44, 47, 77
West Ham Amateur Boxing gym, 93
Westwood, Tim, 96, 97, 106, 108, 109, 165
Whistler, Eric, 19, 20
White, Doris, 11
White, Joe, 11–16; conversion, 13; involvement in Michael's career, 19, 36–7, 66, 71–2, 80, 96–7; takes on father's role, 45; and Michael's injury, 111, 114–17; accompanies Ali on visit, 138; involvement in case against Boxing Board of Control, 157, 160–2, 164, 172
White Hart Lane, 85, 91, 94, 105, 174, 191
Whitechapel Hospital, 175
Woolwich Road, 189, 190
World Boxing Association (WBA), 48, 63
World Boxing Council, 152, 185
World Boxing Organisation, 71, 83, 86, 90–1, 93
Wray, Winston, 39–40

York Hall, 21, 25, 26, 27, 30, 39, 40, 73–4, 77, 81, 165, 193

Zara, 38, 40–1, 43–8; split with Michael, 48, 52, 61–2, 66; visits Michael in hospital, 119–20, 124